George Horton

Songs of the Lowly

And Other Poems

George Horton

Songs of the Lowly
And Other Poems

ISBN/EAN: 9783337181901

Printed in Europe, USA, Canada, Australia, Japan

Cover: Foto ©Thomas Meinert / pixelio.de

More available books at **www.hansebooks.com**

Songs of the Lowly

AND OTHER POEMS.

BY GEORGE HORTON.

CHICAGO:

F. J. SCHULTE & COMPANY, Publishers,

The Ariel Press,

298 Dearborn Street.

CONTENTS.

(iii)

Songs of the Soul.

In Lighter Vein.

Thanksgiving Thoughts.

Translations.

PRELUDE.

The Lost Song.

I PLUCKED a wild flower from the river's brim,
  And drank awhile its faint but fragrant breath,
Then cast it forth upon the wave a-swim,
  And watched it, as I fancied, drift to death.
"'Tis lost," I said; but far adown the tide
  A tempted maiden saw its dainty hue;
She snatched it, kneeling at the water side,
And vowed: "I will be pure, Sweet Flower, like you."
          And I, I never knew.

I plucked a song from out my heart one day,
  And tossed it on the noisy stream of rhyme.
Sadly I watched it slowly float away
  'Mongst thistles, weeds and sprigs of fragrant thyme.
" 'Tis lost," I said, " 'tis lost for evermore,
  Although within my heart of hearts it grew."
And yet, far down beside the reedy shore
  It taught one soul its lesson sweet and true.
          And I, I never knew.

Songs of the Lowly.

SONGS OF THE LOWLY.

No Quarter.

A SAGE once said to me :
    "Of two things warn I thee,
        And one is death.
No skill can stay his arm ;
'Gainst him avails no charm,
        Prayers are but wasted breath.

"When death is standing near,
    All vain is friendship's tear
        Or love's wild woe.
Then turn thee to the wall,
Away from friends and all,
        Only to wait his blow.

"That other thing is want,
    Potent the soul to daunt,
        To curse and blight.
On him that hath not gold
The very sun shines cold,
        And maketh no day bright.

"Friends wail to see thee die ;
    From poverty they fly,
        Nor heed its call.
Who dies hath lived his day ;
The poor can truly say :
        'We have not lived at all.'"

(13)

When Stars Shine.

L OOK ! Daylight's faintest glimmer
      Pales out of earth and sky ;
The serried cliffs wax grimmer,
      Then into darkness fly,
And all the sea's white shimmer
Has dimmer grown and dimmer,
      And darkened far and nigh.

But yonder, yonder, yonder
      Blooms forth each golden star ;
Plucking the night asunder,
      God lights them thick and far,
While all the heavens wonder,
And all the beings under,
      Because such glories are !

Ah ! when joy's sun is going
      And darkness downward rolls ;
When sorrow, blacker growing,
      The lives of men controls —
Then, in God's heaven glowing,
Their tender fierceness showing,
      Bloom out his star-like souls !

The Dead King.

T HE king was dead.   His body lay
      In splendor stern and grim,
While round him fell the dying day,
      Sifted through windows dim.

His sword within his nerveless hand
  Was clasped as when in life,
'Mid battle-clouds, that dreadful brand
  Had flashed and led the strife.

Beside his gray and stately head
  His jeweled crown was set
In readiness, as though the dead
  Had need to wear it yet.

And flags from many a battle-plain,
  Standing about his bier,
Told of rebellious chieftains slain,
  And nations taught to fear.

There, too, steel-clad and tipped with snow,
  Erect and proudly tall,
Were ranged swart sentinels, arow
  Like pillars of the hall.

And all day long, with curious stare,
  And timid, bated breath,
The people gazed upon him there,
  Dead, yet defying death.

Right royal seemed his upturned face,
  For on it lingered still
The majesty of all his race,
  And of his own high will.

The king was dead.   Before God's throne
  A soul stood in the light,—
Abject, misshapen, stripped, alone,
  And shriveled with affright.

Nobles of Heart and of Head.

A NEW order of honor is needed,
    And 'tis time that the old passed away,
For it must and it will be conceded
    That the gods we have now are all clay.
Then hurrah for the man with the hammer!
    Let him smite, in the dust let him tread!
The builders and molders are busy —
    Give us nobles of heart and of head!

"His majesty"— words without meaning,
    For the monarch possesses it not;
"His highness"— the man has a leaning
    To the gutter; in fact, is a sot.
"Most noble "—alas! he is famous
    As a soiler of virtue instead.
O God, give us soon, give us only
    The nobles of heart and of head!

Is an ape, although gilded with riches,
    Worth more than an image of Christ?
Take the old idols down from the niches:
    Too long has their worship sufficed.
Let us bow to the man — he's our hero,
    Though he toil like a slave for his bread.
Let us honor the world's only great ones —
    The nobles of heart and of head.

Hear the prophets with awe, though with wonder;
    Say not, "It is dark," with a sneer:
From the blackest of skies bellows thunder,
    And the heavens then suddenly clear.

It is coming — the day that we long for
(Oh, speed it before we are sped) —
When earth shall pay homage alone to
The nobles of heart and of head !

The Whispering Corn.

HAVE you e'er walked at early morn
Beside a field of stately corn,
Just while the red sun crossed the rim
Of this round world, mist-wet and dim ?
Often have I, if but to hear
Mysterious whisperings far and near.

'Tis just at nature's waking-time,
While hillsides yet are white with rime,
And while the first lark, rising, flings
Dew-spray from off his early wings ;
And now and then a faint sound tells
Where cattle stir and shake their bells.

"Hush," says the corn, "with dog and gun
I see a hunter hither run.
O trembling hare, far inward hie ;
Lie close, O partridge, do not fly."
The hunter lists. It seems to say :
"No game is lurking here to-day."

Sometimes the farmer comes to see,
And then it says : "Here's gold for thee,
Which sun and air and sky and soil
Have gathered to reward thy toil.

Ten thousand sentinels in line
Guard each his gift for thee and thine."

Or if some Dives walks for health,
Worn out with care of useless wealth,
It whispers: "You make gold of tears,
Of hunger, curses, prayers and fears;
But here are alchemists whose gold
Must feed the hungry, warm the cold."

Sometimes, with heavy heart, there goes
A love-lorn swain along the rows:
Then "List!" it lisps; "at husking-bee,
When rafters ring with rustic glee
Of brown-cheeked maids and merry men —
Ah, you shall kiss her, kiss her then."

Thus oft, in low, mysterious wise,
Soft voices from the tall corn rise —
Lulled lispings, as though unknown tongue
Whispered the long lush leaves among —
They tell me secrets sweet and true;
They'll whisper, if you wish, to you.

The Hod-Carrier.

A BOVE him towers, symmetric, lofty, massive,
   Story on story, the unfinished pile.
Here on the walk a moment stands he, passive,
His features stirred by neither frown nor smile.

Windows and niches, arches true and solid,
  Huge blocks of granite, pillars smooth and fair;
These things he heeds not, for his face is stolid,
  And in his eyes no joy there gleams, no care.

Only a toiler he, a bended carrier,
  Who up and down goes slowly all day long;
"He loves his task," say wealthier men, or warier;
  "His mind is dull, his back is broad and strong."

Up now he goes, his load upon his shoulder,
  So little, and the structure is so vast!
Think you he cares how quickly cities moulder,
  How short a time the grandest buildings last?

'Twere useless quite his senses to bewilder
  With history and fate of ancient pile;
What matters it how far great Ramses, Builder,
  Swept with his armies from the fertile Nile?

Above the towns of Uruk, the Chaldæan,
  Sands of the desert sift like sifting snow;
And mighty forests hum a savage pæan
  O'er Toltec cities in Old Mexico.

Deep let them lie! Their glory be forgotten!
  They tell how men were driven in the past.
Their kings are lost, their very stones are rotten,
  But slavery and toil forever last.

Down now he comes. When these fair walls are riven,
  And Ruin's dust drifts over them in scorn,
In some far realm will slaves be bought and driven,
  Will Might still rule in kingdoms now unborn?

Herodotus fished well in priestly gutters,
  Yet on no page the pyramids explains;
But every royal mummy, grinning, mutters:
  "See how we lashed men in our ancient reigns."

Poor, weary toiler! Worse your fate and sadder
  Than that of any slave in ancient day;
'Tis hunger drives you up and down the ladder.
  What tyrant ever could so well dismay?

Think you he knows that kings are no diviner
  Than even he, a dull, down-trodden waif?
That Fortune's pets are made of flesh no finer?
  But no, he sings! Thank God, the state is safe.

My Girl in the Calico Dress.

MY lady is haughty and grand,
  She's a vision of beauty and art;
But I fear that her dainty white hand
  Is softer by far than her heart.
Shall I come as a suppliant near her,   ·
  To be crushed when my love I confess?
Ah, no; there's a fairer and dearer —
  A girl in a calico dress.

My lady has money and style,
  She has dresses and gems by the score,
And lovers to strive for her smile,
  Besides men and maid servants galore;

But my heart sings as loud as a linnet,
  And all envy I quickly repress,
When I hold in my arms just a minute
  That girl in the calico dress.

My lady is traveled and wise,
  She reigns at reception and ball,
She kills, if need be, with her eyes,
  But she blushes, I fear, not at all.
She's a peony, proudly aspiring,
  With no fragrance a lover to bless ;
But a mignonette, sweet and retiring,
  Is my girl in the calico dress.

My lady may freeze when I bow,
  Or as bright as a houri may beam ;
I watch not her moods, for I vow
  That her charms very poor to me seem,
For there's never a maid in all story
  So worthy a prince's caress,
And nothing so fair out of glory
  As my girl in the calico dress !

The Dinner-Pail Brigade.

WHEN morning's chilly grayness
    First glimmers in the sky,
I hear their whistled gayness,
  I see them frayward hie.
From humble street and alley,
  In garb of every trade,

The sturdy heroes sally
  Of the dinner-pail brigade.

Strong-limbed and gallant yeomen,
  Brown-cheeked and fearless-eyed —
The whole wide world has no men
  So worthy of its pride.
The gilded sons of Pleasure,
  And sloths of every grade,
Are but earth's trash; her treasure
  Is the dinner-pail brigade.

They conquer nature's wildness,
  Her mood of rock and thorn,
Until, in fruitful mildness,
  She yields us wine and corn.
And where the wild beast haunted
  They plant the roof-tree's shade —
The pioneers undaunted
  Of the dinner-pail brigade.

The land their cities cover —
  Hives both for drones and bees;
Their white sails flit and hover
  O'er all the merry seas;
They delve where darkly hidden
  The ages' hoards are laid;
Earth has no wealth forbidden
  To the dinner-pail brigade.

O weary, patient brothers,
  This is Time's greatest sin,
That you should drudge for others,
  Should build and not go in;

That thieves should claim the plenty
　　Which God for all has made,
And dole out pittance scanty
　　To the dinner-pail brigade.

Cheer, brothers, cheer, for plainly
　　Dawn blushes in the sky ;
Those who have long prayed vainly
　　Shall learn a battle-cry.
Hold out a little longer :
　　The few shall wax afraid,
Seeing they are not stronger
　　Than the dinner-pail brigade.

For, as the day shines clearer,
　　We see with wiser eyes ;
Despised worths seem dearer,
　　And men look all one size ;
Old values wax romantic,
　　Kings and their creatures fade,
While looms each form gigantic
　　In the dinner-pail brigade !

Found in the Lake.

HERE on this marble slab she lies,
　　Staring with sightless eyes.
Her cheek is white as marble now,
　　And her unwrinkled brow,
Where raven tresses creep and trail,
　　Is more than lily pale.

She's not your loved one.   Gently place
    The sheet upon her face:
She is too frail a thing and fair
    To lie uncovered there
Among the city's unknown dead,
    Upon such horrid bed.
These are mere flotsam from life's sea—
    These ghastly things—but she,
More like some white shell washed ashore
    Amid its ceaseless roar.
And no one knows her.   All that come
    Gaze curiously dumb,
With sickened heart and stifled breath,
    At mystery and death.

She is not yours, nor yours.   Perchance,
    With hungry, eager glance,
Some frightened woman may rush in
    Among these wrecks of sin;
May find what she has come to seek,
    And, with a sudden shriek,
Yea, with a mother's frenzy, fill
    This haunt of gloom and chill.
In such omnipotence of pain
    Death would forget his reign:
Those lips, and that all-hallowed brow,
    So sweetly sacred now,
Where Death has set his seal of snow,
    A mother's kiss would know.
But then, as now, those eyes would stare,
    Unlit by joy or care.

How wonderful is Death !   How dread !
　　If aught could raise the dead —
If any power, below, above —
　　It were a mother's love.

"Found in the lake."   Enough to know
　　That God would have it so.
Ah ! then forbear to question why
　　She deemed it sweet to lie
And let the cooling water swirls
　　Toy with her glossy curls.
All night upon her lily breast
　　The soft waves gently pressed ;
All night they sang upon the shore
　　Low love-songs o'er and o'er ;
All night they rocked her in her sleep,
　　Dreamless, and long, and deep.
"Found in the lake."   What more to say ?
　　Let science stand away.
It matters not if sin's despair
　　Haunted and drove her there ;
More perfect eyes, in clearer light,
　　Will judge her deeds aright.
Then leave a fresh flower with her here,
　　Or, fairer still, a tear.

Go out into the noisy strife
　　Of this great city's life ;
There is no time to think of death,
　　No time for rest or breath,
No time for sentiment or tears,

For aught that soothes or cheers.
Great wagons rattle in the street,
　　The pave is loud with feet,
And shod hoofs clatter on the stones.
　　If any cries or moans
Ring feebly out, the voice of pain
　　Is lost in sounds of gain.
Oh, madness of it all! What meed
　　　Can sate such boundless greed?
White phantom of the morgue, I pray,
　　Haunt me by night and day;
Wide-open eyes, stare into mine,
　　　Reproachful, sad, divine,
Until my heart, no longer dumb
　　In all this roar and hum,
Wakes merciful to any cry
　　　Of hearts that bleed and die.

Another Christmas.

I.

O CHRIST, again we celebrate thy birth.
　　Last night, a sound of sudden carol singing
Came floating in on many a chosen ear;
To-day, the tuneful heavens far and near
Are finely quivering to the distant ringing
Of sweetly chiming bells, or else the sphere
Is shivered by some clamorous crash more near.
In happy homes there is a sound of mirth;

The jolly god, to childish faith so dear,
Has made again his circuit of the earth.
Great country hearths their flames are upward flinging,
Diffusing wide a flickering, rosy glow
O'er waiting board and pendent mistletoe,
And many a scene where joy and plenty dwells;
And prancing steeds come bounding o'er the snow,
Shaking a rhythmic jangle from their bells.

II.

How meet it is that merry Christmas tide
   Should come when Winter, merciless and drear,
Has laid his hand of ice to Nature's side,
   And chilled awhile her kindly heart with fear.

The dusky grape, that erst in Autumn reigns,
   Lurked pregnant, clustered deep in green-leaved vine,
Gleaned in all fields, with song and merry pains,
   Fills vat and cask with rich and mellow wine.

The yellow corn, that caught the very tint
   Of late Autumna's saddest parting smile,
Fills the bulged crib — no need for studied stint,
   Though Winter howls in aimless rage the while.

Then lay the Yule log on its couch of fire;
   Pile high the board with bounteous hand and free;
Fill the old hall; let gray-haired dame and sire
   Mix their shrill merriment with childhood's glee.

III.

There is a scene of woe for every feast,
   And none may laugh but what some other sighs;

Curses with every grateful prayer arise ;
There is no birth but what some heart has ceased.

My ship, perchance, comes safely home to me—
    Hope-laden ; now she nears the quiet port.
    Some other bark, of waves and winds the sport,
Sinks even now beneath a cruel sea.

Within the church, proud Beauty bows her head,
    Or humbly kneels to God in worship meet.
    Without, the shivering wretches on the street
Would gladly give their very souls for bread.

The gods are partial : they give wealth untold,
    With palaces and garnered stores, to some ;
    But others are with silent misery dumb,
Or prate of vengeance, by despair made bold.

IV.

O Christ ! Infinity of Tenderness,
Great Heart of Love itself ! It matters not
Whether thou wert indeed a living truth,
God dwelling with us in our flesh and blood,
Or, as the doubters of this latter day,
Who cannot thrust their fingers in thy side,
Would have the world believe, but an ideal
Shaped by the better yearnings of our race.
Thou art all-worthy of all reverence.
Ah, wise were they who, following first thy star,
Came from far countries in the fabled East
To bow their gray heads to the Babe of Peace.
That star alone can light and warm the world.
And if, e'en while these Christmas bells are chiming,

Gaunt Misery stalks the city's crowded lanes ;
If Famine peers through many a rag-stopped pane
On scenes of squalor and disease within,
Or boldly enters side by side with Death,
It is because the loving Christ, who said,
" Sell that thou hast, and give unto the poor,"
Has in these Christmas feastings been forgot.

To an English Sparrow.

IS it springtime, my pert little sparrow?
  I hear your voice, honest and shrill ;
I see you out there on the narrow
    Promenade of my bleak window-sill.
When the blues came, my spirits to harrow,
You darted in sight like an arrow,
        Piping " Cheer up ! Cheer up !"
So loud on your tiny, blithe quill.

I like you, my brave, saucy Briton ;
  You've a way that has captured my heart ;
And though others your failings may twit on,
  I'm a friend that will e'er take your part.
And, as much as you wish, you may sit on
My sill, which you often have lit on,
        Singing " Cheer up ! Cheer up !"
With a fervor much sweeter than art.

Few people, I know, praise your singing,
  And I own that your harsh vocal powers
Can't compete with the robin's voice ringing
  Every June in the hush morning hours ;

I confess that the lark, upward winging,
And the bobolink's silver throat flinging
    "Bobolink! Bobolink!"
Add a charm to the seasons of flowers.

But when winds of midwinter were blowing,
    And the window-panes rattled with sleet,
And the heavens were gray, and 'twas snowing,
    What became of those visitors sweet?
When we needed them most they were going;
But you stayed, your stout heart overflowing
    In that "Cheer up! Cheer up!"
Which I've heard you so often repeat.

Your enemies say you're a fighter.
    Ah well, what of that? So am I.
I will sing if 'tis darker or lighter—
    You have taught me a gay battle-cry.
When Fortune's against me, despite her
I will wait for the days that are brighter,
    Singing "Cheer up! Cheer up!"
I will fight and will sing till I die.

Song of the Husker.

HARK! far in the field over yonder
    'Tis the corn-husker merrily sings.
Oh, why is he happy, I wonder,
    As the ears in the basket he flings?
As he plucks the dry covers asunder,
And reveals the smooth grain gleaming under,
    And the ears in the basket he flings?

"Ah, here is a plump one, and yellow,
    And here is another as fine,
And that was more fair than its fellow,
    And this has a color divine ; "
So his voice, by the distance made mellow,
    Has a musical cadence and swell, oh !
    A swell and a cadence divine !

Blithe husker, cease not from your singing,
    Though my sadness I cannot control ;
While the ears you are carelessly flinging,
    I think of the state of my soul —
These words in my brain keep a-ringing :
    " What harvest to God am I bringing
    Should death tear the husk from my soul ? "

Smithy Song.

WHEN I am half a-dreaming
    And only half asleep,
When daylight's grayest gleaming
    'Gins through the blinds to peep,
Oh, then I hear the dinging
Of the smithy hammers ringing,
    Ching, *ching*, ching, *ching*,
    Ching, *ching*, ching, *ching*.

At eve, when I'm returning
    From labors of the day,
Their forges yet are burning,
    And still their hammers play,

And oft the smiths are singing
To that measured, merry ringing,
   Ching, *ching*, ching, *ching*.
   Ching, *ching*, ching, *ching*.

Sometimes, with rhythmic bending
   Of bodies to and fro,
They toil in couples, sending
   The sparks out, blow on blow,
One hammer always swinging
The while the other's ringing,
   Ching, *ching*, ching, *ching*,
   Ching, *ching*, ching, *ching*.

O merry anvils sounding
   All day till set of sun!
It is by steady pounding
   That noblest tasks are done.
By sturdy blows and swinging,
That keep the world a-ringing,
   Ching, *ching*, ching, *ching*,
   Ching, *ching*, ching, *ching*.

Love and Love.

I SAW her roll by in her carriage,
   Lolling there in luxurious pride;
She has grown very fine since her marriage,
Though her husband, just then glancing up, he
   Didn't seem at all pleased with his bride.

In fact, he looked angry and jealous ;
  She was fondling a pug at her chin,
With kisses, affectionate, zealous —
Bah ! a woman so fond of a puppy
  Is ugly, though charming as sin !

Just then I espied on the crossing
  A poorly dressed woman and plain,
Caressingly dandling and tossing,
In a manner as gentle as may be,
  Her baby, again and again.

She peeked 'neath the cunning poke bonnet
  At the tiny face nestling within,
And her eyes, as they feasted upon it —
Why, a woman so fond of a baby
  Is charming, though ugly as sin !

Yesterday, To-day, To-morrow.

SHALL we sing till we find ourselves hoary
    Of the years that will no more return ?
Shall we live with the dead but in story,
  And our hearts o'er the past ever yearn ?
Ah, no ! we are sick of the glory of kings and their
    victories gory,
  Their fame and their wisdom we spurn.

Shall we say that our fathers fared better
  In the days of their being than we ?
This age to their time is no debtor —
  We have learned that we dare to be free.

We will strike off each time-honored fetter, in peace
or on battlefields wetter
And more red than the world cares to see.

The past with its tombstones is lying
    In a valley of deepening night;
To-day has less sorrow and sighing,
    Less fear of the future, less blight;
But the voice of To-morrow is crying: "Here the
    white feet of Noon-tide are flying,
And the mountains are splendid with light!"

To the Lake Breeze.

SHOREWARD, fly shoreward, O Breeze of the Lake,
    Over the waters on fleet pinions flee,
Bringing new courage and strength in thy wake,
Joy for the spirits that droop for thy sake,
    Life for the souls that are fainting for thee.

Spread out thy wings like the wings of a gull,
    Widely and whitely, just grazing the wave;
Pause not to frolic, foam blossoms to cull;
Come with sea whispers our fever to lull.
    Speed, gentle goddess, the dying to save.

Come to the toilers of brawn and of brain
    Bravely and willingly winning their bread;
Lighten their labors and lessen their pain;
Haste, ere to hasten be mockery vain —
    Wouldst thou but fondle the cheeks of the dead ?

Come to the army of factory girls,
  Toiling in attic and toiling in shop ;
Bring them a message of cool water-swirls,
Pet the pale faces and toy with the curls,
  Kiss the poor fingers that never may stop.

Visit the victims of cruel disease,
  Dying in hovels or palaces grand ;
Tell them of meadows and leafiest trees,
Lisp them a ditty of wind-wimpled seas,
  Offer thy wine with invisible hand.

Visit the tenement babies to-day,
  Woo them to laughter and brighten their eyes ;
Haste thee ere Jesus shall call them away
Out to the country, and let them in play
  Troop o'er the valleys of dear Paradise.

Hither, fly hither, O Sprite of the Lake,
  Over the billows on white pinions flee,
Bringing fresh courage and strength in thy wake,
Joy for the spirits that faint for thy sake,
  Hope for the souls that are dying for thee.

"Deserving Poor."

DIVES and I on crowded street
    An aged beggar chanced to meet ;
Dives passed by with sterile frown,
And said, to argue conscience down :
" I treat all such with rule unswerving.
How can one know when they're deserving?"

"You're right," I cried, with nodding head
(I toil for Dives for my bread);
But since the mind is heaven-born,
And earthly fetters holds in scorn,
I thought: "That wretch, and many more,
Starve through those words, 'Deserving poor.'"

And then, because I haply knew
How Dives rich and richer grew,
I sneered (in thought): "Such careful alms,
Such nice, discriminating qualms,
Should be observed in rule unswerving
But by the rich who are deserving."

A Corner in Wheat.

(DEDICATED TO A FAMOUS CHICAGO SPECULATOR.)

AN old man sat in a dingy room,
    And a queer old man was he:
He was angle and point from his elbow joint
    To the crook of his awkward knee;
His legs were long, and his face was long,
    And as sad as a face could be;
But his eyes were bright with a dangerous light,
As he hummed with ghoulish glee:
        "Only a penny a loaf,
            Only a penny a loaf;
'Tis only a penny a loaf to the poor,
But it's millions of dollars to me."

He bought all the bread in town one day,
    And the poor man cursed amain ;
But little he cared how the eaters fared —
    He was not in a caring vein.
For the golden wheat, that was made to eat,
    To him was a thing for gain ;
So his features thin wore a ghastly grin
    As he hummed this merry strain :
        " Only a penny a loaf,
          Only a penny a loaf ;
'Tis only a penny a loaf to the poor,
But it's millions of dollars to me."

The poor man sat at his meager board,
    With his wife and children near.
Oh, they saw not, I ween, the phantom lean
    That gazed on their feast with a leer ;
And they never thought that a guest unsought,
    The wraith of an old man queer,
Stood silent and grim in a corner dim,
    And whispered this chorus drear :
        " Only a penny a loaf,
          Only a penny a loaf ;
'Tis only a penny to you, my dears,
And it's millions of dollars to me !"

Behind the Scenes.

BEHIND the scenes the player king
    Wears but a worthless crown ;
He casts it by with careless fling
    And hobnobs with the clown.

The lover, knave, and yokel low,
  The princess in her teens,
Are all one station if you go
  Behind the scenes.

Behind the scenes — two-edged thought
  To prick inflated worth !
Mouth well the lines ye have been taught,
  O great ones of the earth ;
Stride grandly in your rich array,
  Lords, ladies, kings and queens:
There's One that watcheth you alway
  Behind the scenes.

The World in 2000.

THAT'S a wonderful book Edward Bellamy writes
    Concerning the world in 2000,
And all of his readers he greatly delights
    With his tale of the world in 2000.
How sorry we feel that such marvelous sights,
Such heavenly days and such musical nights,
Such moral and mental and physical heights,
    Must all be put off till 2000 !

The spirit of Christ will triumphantly reign
    When time has arrived at 2000,
And selfishness long in its grave will have lain,
    In the year of this era 2000.
Oh, men will be sorry for each other's pain,
Starvation and care will not drive them insane,

And glory shall seem to them better than gain
    When they find themselves safe in 2000.

All men will be equal and all will be free —
    Alas, must we wait till 2000 ?
No rich on the earth and no poor will there be —
    O Time, hasten on tow'rd 2000 !
To God, and God only, will Toil bend the knee,
No strikes and no riots will workmen decree,
And the weak from the strong will have no cause to flee
    When the race has at last reached 2000.

The combines and trusts will be all of them dead —
    But not, I'm afraid, till 2000.
And the last of the lawyers long since will have plead
    Ere that red-letter epoch 2000.
Public place will with honor forever be wed,
And no briber of juries will dare show his head,
For they all will be scorching in Limbo instead —
    Oh my, don't we wish 'twas 2000 !

Obscure authors and artists will all have fair play
    When Eternity's clock marks 2000 ;
For merit alone will expect right of way —
    Alas, 'tis so long till 2000 !
Real poets and writers will shine in that day,
And none will be heard who have nothing to say —
Oh, how would our sonneteers marvel if they
    Should chance to wake up in 2000 !

Many other strange things Mr. Bellamy writes
    Concerning the world in 2000.
I am thinking o' days and I'm dreaming o' nights
    Of the happiness there in 2000.

For the poor are as dogs, snarling over their rights,
While the rich sail above like a bevy of kites,
And our children will long have forgotten the sites
    Of our graves in the days of 2000.

Christian and Pagan.

"BREAD and the circus," hoarsely roared,
    Before Christ came, the Roman horde ;
And pagan Cæsar deemed it wise
To glut its stomach and its eyes.

In this our year of Christian grace
Great Mammon reigns in Cæsar's place.
What is that wail to heaven sped ?
Shame of the ages ! "Work or bread !"

For Want of Breath.

A POOR city babe lay dying one day
    On a ragged and dirty cot,—
Lay quietly gasping its life away
    In a basement squalid and hot.
O God, for a sniff of cool, sweet air—
    Just one for the child and its mother ;
For the heart that bleeds so helplessly there,
    And the babe that must lie there and smother !

The farmer's boy is a cheerful sight
    As he sits on the floor in the sun ;

How he doubles his fists in mimic might,
  How lusty his grief and fun!
Oh, full of life all day is the breeze,
  From the fields of the farmer coming,
For it dallied awhile 'mid leafy trees,
  And awhile where bees were humming.

The fisherman's boy is at play on the sand—
  How sturdy and plump he grows!
There is strength in the grip of his chubby hand,
  And his lips are as red as a rose.
Oh, sweet are the breezes born at sea
  And cradled in white foam flowers,—
Sweet and cool, when waves are like grass on a lea,
  Cool and keen when a tempest lowers.

The babe in the tenement house is dead,
  With none but its mother to weep;
Then lay it to rest in that narrow bed
  Where the sleepers breathe not in their sleep.
O breezes that wander at will alway,
  If ashore or where sea-scud is flying,
There are thousands of poor city babes to-day
  That are smothering, fainting, dying!

Discontent.

O GOD, for the roar of battle,
  For the bayonet's dancing shine,
And the long and merry rattle
  Of musketry down the line!

And oh, for the cannons' crashing
  From the battery on the hill,
And the swords of the horsemen flashing
  As they charge with a right good will!

Away, like a whirlwind driven,
  While a thrill through the sound earth runs;
Away in the smoke, blaze-riven,
  Till we fall on the men at the guns.

And oh, for the broadsides shaking
  The grim old hulls in the bay;
And the boat of the orderly making
  Through the tempest its gallant way!

We are smitten with psychic languor;
  Dry rot is benumbing our minds;
There is in us no love nor anger,
  And our hearts are the hearts of hinds.

We are slaves of lucre and fashion;
  It is custom our age that shapes,
Till we wed without heart or passion,
  And are getting a race of apes.

Our women are all for money;
  Each dupe of us buys his wife;
Their bosoms are wax without honey,—
  They are marble, unloved to life.

There is freedom of speech no longer,
  And scarcely freedom of thought,

For the man with the vault is stronger
Than the soul with an errand fraught.

The rich to the rich are brothers,
And the poor to the poor alone,
And the heart of the hero smothers
Like an acorn beneath a stone.

Then oh, for the trumpets' clamor
And the roll of answering drums,
And oh, for the fire and glamour
With the song of the fife that comes !

For I ween that the first deep thunder
Of the guns like a spell would fall,
And the smoke, ere it crept asunder,
Would enlarge and revive us all.

For the miser would give his treasure
Which he stifles his soul to save,
And the heiress would leap with pleasure
At the deeds of her father's slave.

They are selling ribbons — our heroes,
Our captains are weighing tea,
Our colonels are merchants' zeros,
Our admirals far from sea.

And it's oh, for the muskets' rattle,
And the fife's entrancing call,
For it's better to die in battle
Than never to live at all.

The Outs and Ins.

THROUGH years of mirth and years of woe,
      Through rifts where dawn-light seems to glow,
And on through deeps of awful gloom,
This old world drifts to meet its doom ;
And ceaselessly it hums and spins
To the dreary tune of the Outs and Ins.

The Outs are slaves, who deem this life
A time for labor, care and strife.
Ah, further back than memory runs
Myriads have bowed to greater ones ;
And e'en with History's self begins
The story of the Outs and Ins.

The Ins all dwell in palaces,
And have no cares but those of ease ;
On naught save choicest meats they dine,
And always drink the oldest wine ;
The while the gay world, dancing, spins
To the merry tune of the Outs and Ins.

The Outs are housed on squalid streets,
Where crime with poverty retreats ;
They toil for plenty's scraps and crumbs,
Their children freeze when winter comes ;
The while the sad world moans and spins
To the dismal tune of the Outs and Ins.

The Ins are born of finest clay,
The gods bend down to hear them pray ;

Chance smiles upon them at their birth,
And during all their days on earth
This bright old planet gayly spins
To the jolly tune of the Outs and Ins.

Of coarsest clay the Outs are born —
A heritage of toil and scorn;
And they may curse, or may implore
Our God and all the gods of yore;
But still the dark earth shrieks and spins
To the bitter tune of the Outs and Ins.

Ah me! And so, in life and death,
We cling to Him of Nazareth;
Of blessed Lazarus we tell,
And Dives, dead and gone to hell;
Because this old earth only spins
To the dreary tune of the Outs and Ins.

Consolation.

THERE'S another land and better,
        We are told;
Where the slave shakes off his fetter,
And where worth is never debtor
        Unto gold.

Thither often are we turning
        Weary eyes;
And our heavy hearts are yearning,
Night and day are throbbing, burning
        For its skies.

There that foolish superstition,
　　　Pride of birth,
Finds its sudden demolition,
And our being's final mission
　　　Is of worth.

There the insolence of power
　　　Falls away,
And the proudest soul must cower,
For the spirit takes no dower
　　　From the clay.

Common lives have wondrous splendor
　　　In that light;
For the spirit meek and tender
Puts to shame the king's defender,
　　　Shorn of might.

Natures touched with fires seraphic
　　　Shed their care;
And on peace-girt islands Sapphic,
Far from fretful toil and traffic,
　　　Dream and dare.

Laws through years of wrong descended,
　　　There are changed;
Customs with injustice blended,
Creeds for centuries defended,
　　　Rearranged.

Heaven has solace without measure.
　　　You and I
Should not dream of earthly pleasure,
But should think upon our treasure
　　　In the sky.

The Rag Carpet.

I WON'T oppose Mariar,
   An' stomp around an' fume
About that brustlin' carpet
   For our front settin'-room.
She's kep' her eend up allus,
   I've never seed her shirk ;
She oughter sheer th' pleasure,
   Because she sheered the work.
So if she says a brustlin'
   I'll hev to answer, " Yes,"
Tho' why she thinks 'em purty
   Gits me, I must confess.

I'm awful feared that vain pride
   Has ketched her in its mesh,
An' that she'll starve her sperrit
   An' pomper up her flesh.
She'll want that carpet fetched home
   Wuth mighty how-d'ye-do,
Perched high upon the waggin,
   In all the neighbors' view ;
An' when she gits it nailed down,
   She'll shut the curtains tight,
Fur fear her precious brustlin'
   'Ll ketch a ray o' light.

Oh, yes, I s'pose hereafter
   That our front settin'-room
'Ll be a place o' grandeur,
   O' mystery an' gloom ;

Whenever I go in there
    To look its wonders o'er
I'll have to pull my boots off
    An' leave 'em at the door.
Or p'r'aps she'll lay down long trails
    Of oilcloth everywhere,
Fer me to wander round on
    Ef I should venture there.

Oh well, I hardly blame 'er:
    She's had an uphill time
Sence we sot out together,
    An' life was in its prime.
At first we felt so cheerful,
    So full of vim and hope,
We thought there wa'n't no trouble
    Wuth which we couldn't cope ;
We thought we'd pay off easy
    The morgige on the place,—
But thirty years wuth intrust
    'Twas neck and neck a race.

She done the family washin',
    She pounded, wrung an' rubbed ;
She kep' the house in order,
    She cleaned an' scoured and scrubbed ;
She cooked for all the hired men
    That worked upon the farm —
She's fed a dozen thrashers
    Wuth a baby on 'er arm !
She milked an' done the churnin',
    An' city people found

Her butter was the sweetest
    For miles an' miles around.

She saved up all the meat scraps
    And made 'em into soap,
An', tho' it took the skin off,
    We washed us with the dope.
She done the family sewin'
    An' made the children fine,
She kep' the boys in pants by
    Rejuvenatin' mine.
She showed the children manners,
    An' forced 'em to obey ;
She watched their heads an' noses
    An' learned em' how to pray.

An' now at last the morgige
    Is paid up fair an' square,
I'll give Mariar credit
    An' say she done her share ;
She's earned her right to pleasures
    That's differ'nt from my own,
So I'll take mine in restin',
    While she goes in for tone.
An', anyhow, in this case
    Opposin' wouldn't pay —
She's sot so on the carpet
    She'll have it anyway.

I wonder 'f she remembers
    How thirty years ago
I come each night to spark 'er
    An' hoofed it through the snow ?

That night I popped the question —
　　´By gum, the picter still
Is hangin' round my mem'ry,
　　An' leave it never will !
She set before the fireplace,
　　Red-cheeked and roguish-eyed,
An' what a pile of old clothes
　　Was layin' by her side !

Says she : "Take off your coat, John,
　　I've work enough for you ;
You know you're ornamental,
　　You must be useful, too."
I sat down there beside 'er,
　　My heart beat like a drum ;
Thinks I, the time to ask 'er
　　To-night has surely come.
I tore an' done the cuttin',
　　Mariar sewed the strips,
And not a sound was heard there
　　Except the rips and snips.

An' so 'twas Quaker meetin'
　　Tell purty nigh midnight ;
I thought out twenty speeches,
　　But couldn't start 'em right,
Tell all at once, grown desprit,
　　I hitched my chair up nigher,
An' chokin' back my feelin's,
　　I blurted out "Mariar !"
She dropped her work so sudden,
　　An' turned so deep a red,

I knowed that I was in for't,
  An' had to go ahead.

An' then, somehow or other
  I made 'er understand
I thought she was the best gal
  That nater ever planned.
An' 'fore I parted from 'er
  We'd fixed things up all right
To work together allus
  As we'd begun that night ;
For, bein' sentimental,
  We couldn't help but claim
That life an' makin' carpets
  Was purty much the same.

'Tis us that does the tearin'
  An' sewing up the rags,
But God does all the weavin',
  With care that never lags ;
An' when the carpet's finished,
  An' when we look it o'er,
We'll find what we put in it—
  Not one thing less nor more ;
We'll find it striped and patterned
  An' colored through an' through,
About as we've selected
  The stripes of various hue.

I never hain't regretted
  That night before the fire,
When I set tearin' rags an'
  Jined fortunes with Mariar.

But talk about enjoyment !
  I love to ponder o'er
Them first few years we spent wuth
  That carpet on the floor.
I'll sneak up in the garrit,
  An' think about the past —
The brustlin' carpet cry
  Has struck our house at last !

Babylon is Fallen.

O BEST beloved, who on Patmos' isle
  Heard trumpet voices summon thee on high,
Seeing the gates of glory swing the while,
  What meant that angel with his awful cry ?

"Fallen ! Fallen ! Fallen !
  Is Babylon the great !
Demons and vultures claim her,
  And things of fear and hate."

And tell us, frenzied prophet, our hearts are burning so,
What meant that other angel, so long, so long ago ?

"Woe, woe to Babylon ! In one day comes her doom,
The wrath of God shall smite and utterly consume ;
Mourning and plagues shall come, famine and death
  and fire,
For God the Lord has judged her, and awful is his ire.

"Woe, woe to Babylon ! Her dreadful day is here ;
Far off the kings of earth stand weeping in their fear,

And all the merchants wail and cry in anguish sore
Because their merchandise none buyeth any more.

" Woe, woe to Babylon ! For there no more are sold
Silver and precious stones, fine linen, purple, gold.
Woe, woe the splendid city ! Never there again
Shall any man buy wheat, cattle, or souls of men.

" Woe, woe to Babylon ! For after this dread day
No man on flute or harp within her walls shall play ;
And never shall be heard the voice of bride or groom —
Woe, woe to Babylon ! Behold her fearful doom !"

  I have read it — this wonderful vision ;
   I have studied and pondered it o'er,
  While hummed in my ears the derision
   Of the city's continuous roar.

  Oh, to read it, and drown the soul in it ;
   To gloat, perhaps more than is meet ;
  To swoon o'er it — then in a minute
   To be roused by the sounds of the street !

  Splendid dreamer ! Your promise ecstatic
   Is before me by day and by night,
  But it mocks me the least in my attic
   With windows and shutters closed tight.

Songs of the Heart.

Love.

HOME from the battle plain
     They brought their bravest slain ;

Oh, not with muffled drum
In sadness did they come,

And not with measured tread
As those who bear the dead ;

But like some Bacchic throng,
Madly they rushed along,

Waving their weapons high,
Shouting a battle-cry.

"The city gates throw wide,
Let Victory in," they cried.

Forth poured in gladness then
The women and old men.

"All praise to these," they shout,
"Who put our foes to rout!"

But why that sudden wail,
Turning flushed faces pale ?

It was a voice that said :
"My love is dead, is dead !"

"Nay," quoth a warrior grim,
"Weep not, my child, for him.

In sad and desperate fray
His valor saved the day.

He fell upon the spears
With 'Victory!' in his ears.

He died with sword in hand
The savior of our land.

In fame to live and live,
This life who would not give?"

She answered him and said:
"But he is dead, is dead."

Spake then in bitter pain
The mother of the slain:

"And is he dead, my son,
My beauteous, peerless one?

Yet liefer would I know
That thus he lieth low,

Than if he lived to shame
And blight an honest name!"

"Aye," cried the slain one's sire,
Flushing with sudden fire,

"Glory now hath the boy;
I yield my all with joy!"

Still o'er the stretcher bent,
In grief's abandonment,

That young wife, wildly fair,
Moaning in anguish there;

And this is all she said:
" My love is dead, is dead !"

Out stepped a poet then,
Great, though unknown of men.

" The task," he cried, " be mine
To sing this deed divine —

To tell its beauteous worth
For all the years of earth;

To wed it with sweet sound
While this dark world goes round.

So shall his name outlast
These walls and temples vast,—

Yea, e'en his native land,
Though ages drift like sand."

He ceased. The young wife said:
" But he is dead, is dead !"

Up then a sculptor spake:
" Why sorrow for his sake?

For I will shape his face
In marble's deathless grace;

And I will hew his form
In living curves and warm,

Showing all after days
This hero whom we praise."

The lone one, answering, said :
"But he is dead, is dead."

A painter next spake out :
"Mine be to show war's rout,

Wan hate and fury's spell,—
The night and fire of hell.

And tall amidst the gloom
Our deathless dead shall loom,

Pointing the fearful way
Where fame and victory lay."

And then a gladsome cheer
Rose lusty, far and near,

From all but one, who said :
"My love is dead, is dead !"

Hundreds of years since then,
Full of forgotten men,

Have melted noiselessly,
Like snowdrops in the sea.

The song that poet sung
Yet lives in many a tongue.

The warrior's carven form
Still seems alert and warm.

Men thrill with pride to-day,
Seeing that painted fray.

But, ah! from long ago
There drifts a sound of woe,—

A weary, sad refrain,
Making all glory vain,—

The voice of her who said:
"But he is dead, is dead!"

Court Your Wife.

O MIDDLE-AGED man, I've a word with you,
  As you sit in your office this morn:
Has the worry of life, with its folly and strife,
  Pierced your heart like a festering thorn?
Does the touch of your gold feel too clammy and cold?
  Are you weary of flattery's scorn?

Alas! for the days when the passions of youth
  Burn low in the desolate heart!
When the laughter and tears of our innocent years
  Never more from the sympathies start,
And the hideous mien of indulgence is seen
  'Neath the flattering mantle of art!

Perhaps you've tried friendship, and only have found
  Deception and selfishness rife;

Perhaps you have poured to the needy your hoard,
    To be pricked by ingratitude's knife ;
And perhaps you have been through the whole round of
    sin —
    Did you ever try courting your wife ?

No ?   Then take my advice and I think you will find
    'Tis a pleasure as charming as now.
Follow memory's track till at last you are back
    To the days when you swore to be true —
Yea, dream more and more till she seems, as of yore,
    To be watching and sighing for you.

And when you go home to-night buy a bouquet
    Of the flowers she used to admire ;
Put them into her hand, when before her you stand,
    With a lover-like kiss of desire,
And, oh ! watch her eyes when they ope with surprise,
    And flame up from a smoldering fire !

Then all the long evening be tender and kind,
    Hover near her with eager delight ;
Call her "Darling" and "Sweet," the old titles repeat
    Till her face is with happiness bright—
Try it, world-wearied man, 'tis an excellent plan,
    Go a-courting your dear wife to-night !

First Motherhood.

WHITE as the sheet is her delicate face,
    Girlishly sweet 'mid the linen and lace,
Motherly meet with its new-gotten grace.

Go not away till she opens her eyes ;
Deep in their gray lurks a wondrous surprise,
Bright as the day and as pure as the skies !

Thrilling her breast is the heart of all love,
Keen as the zest of the raptures above,
Tiger's unrest and the fear of the dove.

Bliss that was bred in a transport of pain,
Suffering fled out of ecstasy's reign —
Fled now and dead, though it lived not in vain !

This is a bliss that no words can express ;
Joy such as this they refuse to confess :
Thoughts only miss when we deem that we guess.

Tuned is the heart of the mother full soon ;
Lullabies start there, and many a croon
Sweeter than art and as old as love's boon.

Love's sea is filled to its uttermost deeps ;
If it is stilled how enraptured it sleeps ;
If it is thrilled how it trembles and leaps !

Wonderful power round humanity cast !
All in an hour, and the old life is past ;
Womanhood's flower is expanded at last !

The Old Love.

(WORDS FOR MUSIC.)

OH, let the old love wake again ;
It only sleeping lies ;

Oh, let the old light break again
  From out your dusky eyes.
    Dear Heart, I've wandered lonely
    To many a haven fair,
    And found them sunless only
    Because you were not there.

Oh, let us haste to say again
  Our pledges fond and low,
And let us feel love's day again
  Within our bosoms glow.
    Sweetheart, do you not feel it,
    The tenderness of youth ?
    Your eyes—your eyes reveal it,
    And they are God's own truth !

Oh, let your dear head rest again
  Upon my heart at last,
And when those lips I've pressed again
  One kiss will mock the past.
    True Heart, your graceful lashes
    Are wet, but not with pain,
    For from your eyes there flashes
    Love's sunlight through its rain !

Oh, let the old love wake again ;
  It never should have slept.
Come, let my glad arms take again
  The joy they should have kept.
    Fond Heart, no more of weeping,
    No more the past recall,
    For we are in Love's keeping,
    And love is all in all !

Transformation.

THERE lived a simple country maid
   Years and years ago ;
In summer 'mid the flowers she played,
   In winter 'mid the snow,
And every one that saw her said, with little sigh or shake
      of head :
     "How homely she will grow !"

I saw her in her sweetest 'teen,
   As shy as any dove,
And in her eyes a tender sheen
   Caught from the light above.
" This little maid grows fair," I thought ; "I know what
     all this change has wrought—
     It is the grace of love."

A year sped round, and I once more
   Within her presence stood.
Fairer she seemed than e'er before,
   Stately and brave and good.
And when I looked I said, " I know that grace which
     now hath changed you so—
     The grace of motherhood."

When next I saw her, at the change
   I gazed with bated breath.
Her face was white and rare and strange,
   Like one's who slumbereth,
Dreaming of things unsaid, unsung as yet by any mortal
     tongue—
     That was the grace of death !

Black-Eyed Alice.

BLACK-EYED Alice was so stately,
   Of such queenly presence she,
That each night when she sedately
   Gave her finger-tips to me,
Chilled by such a haughty bearing
   I essayed no greater daring.

E'en my looks I long dissembled,
   Fearing that too bold they were,
And my voice, that somehow trembled
   As I parted late from her,
As I said "Good-night," and after,
   Cursed her good-night's careless laughter.

But, alas for stately Alice
   And the seeming haughty bearing,
For the black eyes' tender malice
   Stung me once to sudden daring.
Dear black eyes! that then belied her,
   As I trembled there beside her.

Suddenly her bearing altered,
   And a coyness sweet possessed her,
While the little "No" she faltered,
   Conscious of my wish confessed her.
Ah, that "No!" Could I resist her?
   When she faltered "No!" I kissed her.

Eyes of True Love.

SWEETHEART, do you remember how
   One evening, years ago,
I held you where I found you, with both my arms around
      you,
   Close to my heart as now,
    And kissed you, dearest, so, and so ?

The golden summer sun had set,
   But through the sifting gray
There blushed a purple glimmer that dimmer grew and
      dimmer,
   While low to westward fluttered yet
    Torn banners of the fleeing day.

A subtle sadness filled the hour,
   Or so it seemed to me,
Which flitting breezes often vainly essayed to soften,
   With scents from many a garden flower,
    And many a rifled locust tree.

I spoke of love in awkward wise,
   And waited as one might
To hear God's answer given awarding hell or heaven,
   And you—you said: "Look in my eyes."
    I looked, and lo! there came no night.

Dear stars of love, that all these years
   Have beamed on me alone !
Bright suns, that cheer me whether 'tis fair or cloudy
      weather,
   And paint with rainbow hues our tears;
    Deep wells of truth—look up, my own !

The Old Fireplace.

YOU may talk about your furnace fires
  That warm your city homes,
And tell me how the heat aspires,
  And through the building roams ;
'Tis handy, I'll admit, to push
  A little iron wheel,
And let the ghost of summer out
  Around the room to steal.
      But oh, I'd love to see once more
        My father's big fireplace ;
      To hear the old logs sing and roar,
      And watch the dodging sparks outpour
        And up the chimney chase !

Your modern grate's a nice affair ;
  When full of anthracite,
It lends the room a pleasant air
  On any winter's night.
The glowing coal's a flower-bed —
  Lilies and crimson pinks,
And 'mong them many an elfin eye
  Peeps through, and winks and blinks.
      But oh, I long to see once more
        My father's old fireplace ;
      To watch the shadows flicker o'er
      My mother's whitely sanded floor,
        And round the ceiling race !

These patent parlor stoves are fine,
  And charm away the chill,

With windows whence the light may shine
The room with cheer to fill.
Some people love to boast about
Our stylish modern ways,
And thank the Lord who cast their lines
In these progressive days;
But oh, that I might be once more
Beside the old fireplace!
To see the fleet-winged flames upsoar
And watch the flashes on the floor
Entwine and interlace.

Hearty and jovial fires were those
I loved so when a boy.
They tinted darkness like the rose
And warmed the heart with joy;
They chuckled in an undertone,
They cackled, whistled, laughed;
They burned so bright, the cares of life
Flew upward in the draught!
And oh, I'd love to be once more
Beside the old fireplace;
To drowse upon the sanded floor
And find my mother bending o'er
With love-light on her face.

The Sweet Girl Graduate.

ANGEL in a robe of white,
Standing there,
With a kiss of yellow light
On your hair:

By the vermeil of your cheek,
By your eyes that more than speak,
By all graces shy and meek,
        You are fair !

You have learned to *"parlez vous,"*
        I suppose,
And have read some Latin, too,
        Verse and prose ;
You have wept Francesca's woe,
Read your Emerson, I know,
And can tell us where the Po
        Flowed and flows.

You, mayhap, have deeper gone
        E'en than this,
Though I would not wager on
        What you wis.
Yet, perhaps, your books among
You have learned, although so young,
How to write the English tongue—
        Learned miss !

Read us now the essay, dear,
        Erudite ;
We will listen, never fear,
        With delight ;
For we know 'twill be a treat,
Wisdom's choicest, richest meat—
And you look so very sweet
        All in white !

Take your parchment with the rest ;
        School is out.

Let no fear disturb your breast,
          And no doubt.
Whether you are dull or wise,
There is something in those eyes
Sure all critics to surprise
          And to rout.

Beauty no diploma needs,
          Earned or bought.
Beauty of itself succeeds,
          As it ought.
'Tis the thing we all adore,
That we strive for more and more —
You are music, art and lore,
          Heaven-wrought !

Like a Rose.

(*À la* Austin Dobson.)

I CAN see her standing yet,
          Dewy-eyed,   .
As she stood that summer morn
          At my side ;
It is not so long ago
That I parted from her so ; .
Yet the gulf is fixed, I know,
          Deep and wide.

Down the garden path we walked
          To the gate,
And I begged her, "Ah, my own,
          Name the date."

But she answered : "No, my dear,
'Tis your fickleness I fear —
I will try you for a year —
    You must wait."

Grief was on my features then
    Written plain,
For she said : "I'm sorry, dear,
    For your pain.
Take this little rose, I pray ;
It will wither in a day.
But my love for you for aye
    Shall remain."

Love is sometimes sweet and sure,
    I suppose ;
Who would not have faith in such
    Vows as those ?
But, alas ! I'm forced to rue
That they were but semi-true,
For her love has withered too,
    Like the rose.

See, I let it flutter thus
    To my feet.
Ah, 'twas summer when its charms
    Were complete.
Save it not : my heart is set,
For 'tis wise I should forget,
And its perfume lingers yet,
    Faint and sweet.

A Christmas Eve Sermon.

CEASE, little one, your laughter,
　And climb upon my knee ;
Be patient, dear, till after
　You've listened well to me ;
For now a tinge of sadness should mingle with the
　　gladness
　　Of this your Christmas glee.

Our hearth is gayly roaring,
　Flame-elfs dance round the room ;
We see the red sparks soaring,
　For us the fire-flowers bloom.
So bright we are, and cheerful, we think not of the
　　tearful,
　　And those who dwell in gloom.

For while you roam, a-sleeping,
　In dreamland, fair and bright,
A thousand children, weeping,
　Will dread the coming light ;
And pain will leave its traces on many tear-wet faces
　　Through all the dreary night.

Then in your prayers remember
　The dear Christ to implore
For those whom this December
　Brings grief, and nothing more.
And, oh ! forget not, darling, those who must hear the
　　snarling,
　　Gaunt wolf paw at the door.

Perhaps—who knows?—the pudgy,
　　Quaint driver of reindeer
May down our chimney smudgy
　　With such a big load steer,
That you may have the pleasure of giving from your
　　　treasure
　　Some poor child's heart to cheer.

This time should never find us
　　To our own pleasure wed;
It should of Christ remind us,
　　Whose heart for others bled—
Hang up your little stocking, for sleep your lids is
　　　locking,
　　And run away to bed!

Grandmother.

GRANDMOTHER sits before the fire
　　Knitting with hands that never tire;

Toiling as though, in sooth, she thought
Mittens and socks could not be bought.

A quaint old dame to me she looks,
Like those one sees in children's books:

With specs on nose, with wrinkled face
Framed neatly in a cap of lace,

From morn till night she's sitting there
Rocking away in her rocking-chair.

Grandmother's room and treasures are
Seen through the door that's half ajar.

We leave it open nights to keep
Her nice and warm while she's asleep.

A ponderous thing her bedstead seems,
Carven of solid walnut beams;

Children mistake it in the dark
(Or say they do) for Noah's ark:

Upon it rests a feather bed,
With feather pillows at the head.

A wondrous couch! And every whit
Of four feet six to top of it;

To me a marvel long it's been
How gran'ma ever scrambled in.

And in that room she keeps a score
Of books that people read no more.

Of these, I think, she loves the best
That dream of glory, "Baxter's Rest."

And next — old people are so queer —
She holds dull Martin Tupper dear.

Jane Austen's tales she keeps there, too,
And other authors not a few,

But little suited to these days
Of stilted verse and foreign craze.

But hold, one book she has which I
Must not too hastily pass by:

A quaint edition of God's Word,
Adorned with pictures most absurd.

Let those who open have a care!
Old Clutie hides in ambush there.

His form the front fly-leaf adorns,
Authentic, tricked with hoof and horns.

His garb suggests an ancient sport,
Picked from the last King George's court;

And such you might imagine him,
But for his tail so long and slim,

That makes a loop or two before
Its barbed end rests upon the floor.

'Tis many a year now, I am told,
Since gran'ma read this Bible old.

Not that our modern ways destroy
At all her faith in the "Old Boy,"

But, as she puts it, with a smile,
"The picture's clothes are out of style."

Speaking of smiles, grandmother's face
Is their continual dwelling-place.

And when the babe, who oft o'erflows
With sayings wiser than she knows,

Cries: "Gran'ma don't look cross nor sad,
And yet she's wrinkled awful bad,"

The dear old soul makes answer mild :
" My wrinkles come from smiling, child."

Much more, if need were, I could tell
Of this old dame we love so well :

For instance, there's the flower-spot
Each spring returning sees her plot.

She studies o'er it hours and hours,
But always picks the self-same flowers :

Pansies and morning-glories fine,
Sunflowers, like sentries in a line ;

A little patch of four-o'clocks ;
Some " hens and chickens " in a box.

And you'd be more than touched, I weet,
To hear her sing low — low and sweet :

" I'm Sitting by the Stile, Mary,"
Or oftenest, " My Ain Country."

But if you'd like to see and know
This queer old lady I love so,

Come to my house.   You'll find her there
Rocking away in her rocking-chair.

But don't put off your visit, pray ;
She sometimes hints at going away.

First Sweethearts.

ONE song for the first sweethearts,
Ah me!
For the loves of our boyhood days;
Our tender regret for them never departs,
Nor fades in oblivion's haze.

One song for the sweet little girls,
Ah me!
For the faces all lily and pink;
For the dears that wore pinafores, ribbons and curls,
Whom we loved to insanity's brink.

There was tenderness free from guile,
Ah me!
And the faith of our earliest youth;
When the buds of affection oped first at a smile,
And thrived in the sunshine of truth.

My sweetheart is dead years and years,
Ah me!
And yours to another is wed;
But we'll sigh for them both, and we'll mingle our tears,
For to us they are both of them dead.

If they were our wives, do you think,
Ah me!
They would still be the girls that we knew?
Will heart-freshness outwear the lily and pink?
Has it ever remained a life through?

For if such a thing were in life,
        Ah me !
And there were no drifting apart,
Each man would be happy, I ween, with his wife,
    His dear little first sweetheart.

Aftermath.

(OF GETTYSBURG FIELD.)

FRIENDS with a love that grows,
    Friends with a love sublime,
That deeper, broader flows,
    And flows to the end of time.

"The aim of war is peace."
    And love to peace belongs ;
Let peevish bickerings cease ;
    The brave forget their wrongs !

Where once, in war's eclipse,
    Cannon, with fevered breath,
With hot and trembling lips,
    Roared their hoarse threats of death,

The heroes of the fray,
    The men who shed their blood,
Have plighted — Blue and Gray —
    Eternal brotherhood ;

Have laid their hatreds there,
    Deep as the buried slain —

Shame on the ghouls that dare
  To dig them up again !

Have found forgotten graves,
  With sweet flowers overgrown —
Why search where green grass waves
  For some uncovered bone ?

No spot upon this earth
  Has seen more glorious hate ;
No spot has greater birth
  Of love made consecrate.

Oh, that some prince of song,
  Some wizard of men's tears,
Would float its fame along
  The muddy stream of years !

Would sing, in worthy strain,
  How the mad battle surged
When Pickett o'er the plain
  His brave Virginians urged —

Earthquake and thunder thrill,
  Lightning, that blazed and leapt,
And then, from hill to hill,
  The living cyclone swept ;

How gallant Armistead,
  With cheeks and eyes aflame,
Rushed, with uncovered head,
  Into the arms of Fame !

How Cushing, pierced to death,
  Clung to his cannon hot,
Shouting, with dying breath :
  "I'll give them one more shot."

Splendid they were as foes,
  Heroes, both wrong and right ;
Shame on the one that throws
  Mud at their flag of white !

Idle are words of hate,
  Useless are taunts and slurs ;
The chariot wheels of Fate
  Will crush all wayside curs.

Since this round world was bowled,
  It has smooth and smoother whirled ;
And before the sun grows cold
  Love will have warmed the world.

The Last Straw.

I DIDN'T feel so very old,
    When nurse come, all a-titter,
An' handed me, to kiss 'n hold,
  A fuzzy, squallin' critter.
The first time one's a daddy, he
  Somehow don't stop to figger ;
He feels ez awkward's he can be,
  An' stouter, better, bigger —
    But not so very old.

I didn't feel so very old
    When first my teeth went thumpin',
Nor when the dentist took a-hold
    An' never left a stump in.
False ones are clumsy, but they'll pass ;
    Jest do a little grinnin',
Standin' before the lookin'-glass,
    And you'll appear quite winnin'—
        An' not so very old.

I didn't feel so very old,
    When first I had a symptom
Of rheumatiz each spell o' cold ;
    Of course, I knew I limped some,
But in these days folks live so fast,
    'Twixt gold and pleasure-huntin',
Their youthful spryness doesn't last,
    An' lots of folks do gruntin'
        Who 're not so very old.

But now I'm feelin' kind o' old —
    Perhaps I hadn't oughter,
But in this letter I am told,
    "Your daughter's got a daughter."
Oh my, how swiftly, one by one,
    The years sneak 'round behind us :
We only think how fast they run
    When Life and Death remind us —
        Yes, yes, I'm gittin' old !

Autumn Leaves.

IN early youth I loved a village maid,
    And lived in ecstasy for days and days.
Her dainty feet through all my future strayed ;
    Her bright eyes beamed in all its purple haze.

My love was fierce in tenderness and joy ;
    It was a thing divine, and thrilled my soul,
Until it changed me from a foolish boy
    To one who deemed the world in his control.

Waking, I wandered in a realm of dreams,
    And builded castles by a distant sea,
Kissed everywhere by mellow glory gleams ;
    And she was queen, and dwelt with love and me.

Brief was the fickle summer of our bliss,
    For cruel Fate our hearts asunder tore.
One autumn eve we parted, with a kiss,
    And went in other ways forevermore.

Ah me ! I know not what my life had been,
    Lit by the tender lovelight of her eyes.
Perhaps I still, as then, had wandered in
    The outskirts of God's blessed paradise.

I only know that oft, when leaves are red,
    Vague loneliness comes o'er me like a spell,
And then I see her stand, with drooping head,
    And hear again her sweet voice say " Farewell."

The Neglected Grave.

ONE evening, after Decoration day,
　I lingered when the rest had gone away,
And sadly strolled among the graves alone,
With fresh-cut flowers by loving hands bestrewn.

How many thoughts within my heart awoke!
Of keenest memories the roses spoke;
The lilies breathed of peace and joy above,
And every tiny blossom whispered "Love."

Then suddenly I felt around me there
The presence of the dead, benign and fair,
And in my heart the glad conviction grew
That all our earthly love they saw and knew.

I turned away to quit the holy place,
When, lo! a vision of angelic grace,—
A beauteous picture ne'er to be forgot,—
Beamed on my sight and held me to the spot.

A little child was standing by a grave;
Her hair fell free in many a golden wave,
And when she looked I saw within her eyes
Tears, mixed with smiles, like rain in sunny skies.

"Are you not lost, my little maid," I said,
"So late amid the dwellings of the dead?"
　In sweetest, saddest tones she answered me:
"Here's one that hasn't any folks, you see.

"'The only grave that every one passed by,
　And when I thought of it it made me cry.

The one there by the willow-tree is ours,
Covered so thick with all those pretty flowers.

"My Uncle Frank's—he'll never care, I know,
If some of his upon this one I throw.
When he was shot, I've heard my gran'pa say,
And dying on the field of battle lay,

"He made the doctor leave him where he fell
And take some other man who might get well."
She ran, and soon her chubby arms were filled
With flowers that on the friendless mound she spilled.

Her mission done, the little maid I bore
Safe in my arms back to her mother's door,
Kissed her good-by, and thought how wondrous fair
The Christ-love mirrored in the child-love there.

Oh, those neglected graves! weed-covered mounds,
Lone slabs and trenches on old battle-grounds.
Let us remember them wherever known,
In His dear name that loveth all His own.

A True Story.

'TWAS just at eve, long years ago,
    A little girl lay dying,
And they who soon would miss her so
    Stood by her, softly crying.
They said, "She's gone." But soon her eye
    Beckoned her father near,
And when he bowed his head more nigh
She whispered low, with latest sigh—
    "Be a dood man, papa dear."

God knows : perhaps the spotless soul,
   Part way toward glory winging,
Turned earthward from its heavenly goal
   This precious message bringing.
Perhaps so tender was her love
   For those remaining here,
It brought her, like a blessed dove,
Back with these words of peace and love—
   " Be a dood man, papa dear."

A change came o'er the father then,
   Subduing him and taming;
No more he sought, with sinful men,
   Resorts of vice and gaming.
For always, after that sad day,
   To wicked taunt and jeer
He answered : " I'll not go astray.
I hear my girl in heaven say—
   ' Be a dood man, papa dear.' "

Bedtime.

OUR little Lucy was a tease,
   A curly-headed bother,
And yet she couldn't help but please
   Kind-hearted old grandfather.
He shared her sorrow and her play,
And was her faithful slave all day,
   From early morn till bedtime.

She had him up and dressed before
   The humble bees were humming,

And kept him wide awake till o'er
   The lea the cows were coming.
Such walks they took! such romps they had!
That little rogue was never glad
   When darkness came and bedtime.

But when the summer twilight fell
   On wood and fragrant meadow,
And sleepily old Blossom's bell
   Clanged in the purple shadow,
Grandfather'd seek his big arm-chair
And call from 'neath the hopvines there:
   "Come Lucy, dear, it's bedtime."

Into his lap she'd scramble fast,
   And there with sleep would wrestle,
Until the curly head at last
   Would on his bosom nestle.
How gently have I seen him rise
And say, with love in voice and eyes,
   "Mamma, it's Lucy's bedtime."

One night he called her not; but still
   And motionless was sitting,
Though cried the plaintive whippo'will,
   And bats went dimly flitting.
But when the red moon fired the dew,
Across the lawn to him she flew
   With, " Grandpa, why, it's bedtime.'

Oh, Youth and Age! Oh, Death and Life!
   One stopped and one beginning;
This side and that of all the strife,

The praying and the sinning.
Mother, with startled cry, draws near,
Then murmurs, half in awe, half fear:
" Ah, yes, my child, it's bedtime."

What will he Grow?

L ANGUOROUS croon of a low lullaby,
   Hitherward wafted from vine-hidden door,
Teach me, a saddened and worn passer nigh,
   Some of your wonderful music and lore.

Mother is cooing her baby asleep —
   Tenderly cooing, and rocking her own.
Bright little eyes, how they twinkle and peep !
   Soft is the ditty, but slumber has flown.

   " Sleep, my precious ; sleep, my treasure ;
      Father's sailing o'er the sea,
     Bringing joy that has no measure —
      Coming home to you and me.

   " Sleep, my precious ; cease from crying —
      He will kiss his baby soon ;
     For I see his white sails flying,
      Framed all in a silver moon.

   " Sleep, my precious ; there's a trailing
      Path of glory on the sea ;
     In it father's safely sailing —
      Sailing home to you and me."

Faint now and fainter the lullaby song
   Grows, with its burden of hope and of faith ;

Doubt overtakes me, and follows along,
  Whispers and leers like a hideous wraith.

Mother is cuddling her baby in bed,
  Gazing upon him with love-hungry eyes.
What will he grow ?   Were it better, instead,
  Mother should strangle him there where he lies ?

Yellow Fever Heroes.

WAR has no heroes : madness comes
    When bugles call, sweet-voiced and clear,
    And when the startled warriors hear
The sudden roll of answering drums.

War has no heroes : madness grows
    When steel is flashing in the sun,
    And when, through rising dust-clouds dun,
The battle forms, in serried rows.

When bullets whistle merry strains,
    And foamy steeds dash riderless,
    Cowards forget themselves and press
Into the fray — then madness reigns.

Heroic deeds of peace sing I,
    Noblest and grandest of all time ;
    Devotion perfect, faith sublime,
Courage that scorns to faint or fly.

Yea, bring war's vaunted great ones forth,
    And all their bloody deeds rehearse ;
    In pale-faced nun and gentle nurse
I see a loftier, truer worth.

No glory clamor, no pretense
Is round their quiet courage flung
Who go with Christ-like zeal among
The flying shafts of pestilence.

They die, if need be ; not with shout
Of victory with latest breath :
Pierced by the poisoned darts of Death,
Their lives ooze slowly, sadly out.

Let scornful pessimist be dumb,
For now I know the earth will drift
Through gloom of ages into rift
And glow of fair millennium.

To a Plain Woman.

A BUBBLE cast upon a boundless sea
Of rhyme; one note struck from a tuneless lyre,
And heeded not by those that nearest be ;
A child's song uttered in a mighty choir;
This verse may not to better fate aspire.
Oh, that it were some gift to offer thee,
Some rare stone's heart, aglow with priceless fire,
Potent with hidden charms, unknown to all save me.

Such gift is not in all my little store ;
The eager, nimble fingers of Defeat
Have turned too oft my heap of treasures o'er,
And culled therefrom all worthy things and meet.
Oh, that I might, then, in this lone retreat,
Enwrap thy name, as Laura's erst of yore,

In quaint thought-sheaflets, keeping green and sweet,
  When I have silent been, long since, forevermore.

Beauty is vain from Flattery's senseless mead,
  In all remembered and forgotten song,
Since love-lorn shepherd first on slender reed
  Piped madness sweet some ancient brook along.
Let me, presumptuous, leave this servile throng,
  Awhile, at least, from Beauty's shackles freed;
I cast them from me once, with impulse strong,
  And lo, no bruise was left, no scar to smart and bleed.

Fair Cytherea,—thou whose form divine,
  A splendid flower, unfolded on the main —
Unfolded, and was mirrored in the brine,—
  I know thee, and I know thy fickle reign;
Unseemly, reckless, have been all thy train,
  From her who melted jewels in her wine
Down to that so-called Lily, soiled and vain —
  Ah, slandered flower, such grace, such purity is thine!

I fancy that dear Florence Nightingale
  To dying eyes, and eyes that looked despair—
Although her cheeks were fever-sunk and pale —
  Seemed wondrous sweet, and ravishingly fair;
And thou, my own, these eyes, in joy and care,
  Have found thee decked with graces that avail
To make thy presence exquisite and rare —
  Fragrant from hidden sweets that Time may ne'er
    assail.

Old Mother Goose.

I WILL name you the greatest of all poetesses,
And you'll own that I'm right when I do,
Though you probably couldn't in twenty-five guesses
Hit her name, should I ask it of you.
Mrs. Hemans? or Sappho? or sweet 'Liza Cook?
Mrs. Browning? the Carys? No use;
It is strange you're so dull when you've all seen her
book—
I am thinking of Old Mother Goose.

But should you dispute me, a million bright pleaders
Will join, I am sure, on my side,
And we'll claim that no poet has more loving readers
And none reputation so wide.
How the little ones struggle, when sly spider Sleep
Has them all tangled up, to get loose!
For they want, just as long as their pretty eyes peep,
"One more story from Old Mother Goose."

Of her poems, how many are great masterpieces!
Not one, but a dozen at least.
There's Old Mother Hubbard, whose trouble increases;
Jack Sprat and his sensible feast;
And the woman who ran her head foolishly through
Matrimony's untieable noose,
And settled for life in that wonderful shoe—
They are all there in Old Mother Goose.

Then her fancy's a fountain of pleasure unfailing,
And her Pegasus often mounts high;
In the case of the witch who on brooms went a-sailing

She takes us clear up to the sky.
And those three learned men who a-cruising would go,
    And thought a tub fitted their use,
Their whole trip is left to the fancy, you know —
    Such a shrewd one is Old Mother Goose.

Dear poet of babyhood ! Oft in the city
    Your verses are thought of, I wean ;
When the care-worried merchant hums softly some
        ditty,
    'Tis his mother's face rises serene.
How pure were the counsels that long lost one gave !
    For his faults he can find no excuse,
When he visits in spirit a far-distant grave,
    Led thither by Old Mother Goose.

Ah me ! where's the hardened and worldly-wise sinner
    (And we all of us sin less or more)
Who'd refuse to again be a little beginner,
    Learned only in childhood's sweet lore ?
How many could start on a far better way,
    Or their gifts put to worthier use,
Could they find themselves back in that innocent day
    When they marveled at Old Mother Goose !

An Idyl of California.

COME, sit awhile beneath this spreading arbor
    Of lusty fig and intercreeping vine ;
My heart no other guest save love shall harbor
    While thou art mine —
            Boy, bring wine.

No classic maid art thou — just modern Alice ;
   Yet fair enough to turn despair to joy.
Come now, charm from me, with your black eyes' malice,
   The world and care's alloy —
           That wine, boy.

Fair Lalage, however sweetly smiling,
   Beamed not on Horace with such eyes as thine ;
Dark Amaryllis ne'er was so beguiling,
   Nor Hero so divine —
           Drink, drink wine.

Ah ! what is this ? A fleeting cloud of sadness,
   That love their hearts may never more annoy ?
Be wise, then, girl, and seize life's transient madness
   Ere hungry Time destroy —
           More wine, boy.

Perhaps — who knows ? — when we are dead, and scattered
   Through earth and sea and heaven, far and fine,
Your name, like those of others wooed and flattered,
   May live in some sweet line —
           Ah, that wine !

But now's our turn for love and laughter, Alice ;
   Be coy, I pray you ; but be not too coy.
The ages offer us their thrilling chalice —
   'Twill shatter ere we cloy —
           More wine, boy.

Dark blood peeps through your smooth skin's lily whiteness,
   'Twixt ruddy lips your teeth gleam, all a-line ;

Sunshine is woven in your brown hair's brightness.
  Ah, which is hair ?   Which shine ?
          Drink more wine.

These things will fade, and what will follow after ?
  Alas, that Fate must use us for a toy !
But now's the time that wine and love and laughter
  Should all our thoughts employ —
          Bring wine, boy !

A Young Nun.

WITHIN the convent grim and gray,
    And ivy-grown,
She liveth on, from day to day,
    Life's monotone.

She leaveth oft the ancient pile
    And passeth by.
Yet I have never seen her smile
    Nor caught her eye.

Her hands are very white and small,
    And those who know
Say that on Fever's brow they fall
    Like flakes of snow.

They say her voice is soft and sweet
    In Sorrow's ear,
Wooing the soul to Mary's feet
    From doubt and fear.

Ah me!   And yet her youthful face,
   Clad though it be
In cold religion's saintly grace,
   Is fair to see.

Her eyes, so modestly cast down,
   So introspect,
Could light a smile or arm a frown
   With dire effect.

'Tis just such orbs that steadiest burn
   With passion's fire;
Can all the tears in Virtue's urn
   Quite quench desire?

Her mouth is red, and shaped for bliss;
   It seems a loss
That it should only kiss and kiss
   Her rosary cross.

Oh, Little Nun!   Thou art too fair!
   It had sufficed
If one less sensuously rare
   Had wed thy Christ.

The devil oft in form of saint
   Entraps the eyes;
Thou art a soul without attaint
   In devil's guise!

Growing Reconciled.

WHEN her husband first departed
    Widow Blacke was very sad ;
You'd have thought her broken-hearted,
    Such a mournful way she had.
        Oh, the sorrow of her sighing !
        Oh, how wearily she smiled !
        People thought : " With grief she's dying,
        She will ne'er grow reconciled."

Now, if you will closely scan her,
    You, perhaps, may note a change ;
Something in her dress or manner
    Out of sorrow's widest range.
        Widow Blacke's but three and twenty —
        Why, she's nothing but a child ;
        One year's mourning is a plenty.
        Is she growing reconciled ?

Seems to me the ashy whiteness
    On her cheek is giving way
To a hue of healthy brightness,
    Waxing deeper day by day.
        Gossips say, and it's a pity,
        That her cheeks with paint are piled ;
        Widow Blacke is very pretty —
        Is she growing reconciled ?

Near the grave where Blacke reposes
    I was strolling yesternight
And I spied a bunch of roses
    Near the headstone — withered quite.

Roses are so very fleeting !
  So are griefs, if deep or mild,
And I couldn't help repeating,
  " Is she growing reconciled ? "

Then her mourning, I'm not sure
  Whether pride or grief it shows ;
Mourning's so becoming to her,
  Such a foil for pink and rose !
    Who's that promenading yonder ?
      Widow Blacke and Major Wilde ?
    No ! It is, though, for a wonder :
      She is growing reconciled.

Chansonette.

YOUR love is far dearer, Sweetheart,
  To me than your beauty or grace ;
And your smiles I hold nearer, Sweetheart,
  Than the charms of your wonderful face.

'Tis your kiss that entrances, Sweetheart,
  Not the red of your ravishing lips ;
And your passionate glances, Sweetheart,
  Throw the light of your eyes in eclipse.

For the world without asking, Sweetheart,
  Your grace and your beauty may see ;
But 'tis I who am basking, Sweetheart,
  In your love, and that's only for me !

The Widower.

HE dreams : Her head upon his breast
  Lies cozily and well at rest.
He feels her bosom's fall and rise
And drinks the perfume of her sighs.

He wakes : Against the rattling pane
He hears the wan and ghastly rain —
Ah God ! He thinks of how she lies,
And shuts no more his tearless eyes.

Love's Opportunity.

TWO lovers by the old front gate,
  So young and all alone !
The village clock tolls : Late ! Late ! Late !
  Twelve times in solemn tone.
      " No ! No !"
A deep voice says aloud,
      " Sweetheart, don't go
Till the moon goes under a cloud."

The Queen of Night rides high in space,
  Serenely bright and fair ;
Her kisses gild the young swain's face,
  The maiden's glossy hair.
      'Tis late,
And all their vows are vowed :
      Why wait, and wait,
Till the moon goes under a cloud ?

The fair girl's dewy lips repeat :
"Good night is not good-by."
But love in youth is very sweet,
And village maids are shy.
Dear one,
With head so sweetly bowed —
Don't run, don't run,
Till the moon goes under a cloud.

Old Man Thurman.

[Allen G. Thurman usually addressed his wife as "Sweetheart."]

A SONG for old man Thurman,
And sing it clear and strong.
His life has been a sermon,
Now let it be a song.
And this shall be its burthen,
To give us greatest joy —
He calls his old wife "Sweetheart,"
And loves her like a boy.

There is no fairer story
In all our nation's life ;
No better, purer glory
In all its peace and strife.
True is that man, and steadfast,
Fine gold, with no alloy,
Who calls his old wife "Sweetheart,"
And loves her like a boy !

Who cares for his position
  On questions of the day?
He has a higher mission —
  A nobler part to play!
Smiling and patient ever,
  Though Age and Pain annoy,
He calls his old wife "Sweetheart,"
  And loves her like a boy! ·

A fig for flowery diction
  Or specious eloquence!
A fig for all the fiction
  Of wealth and vain pretense!
Here is a man whose glory
  No envy can destroy —
He calls his old wife "Sweetheart,"
  And loves her like a boy!

We well could spare the splendor
  And tinsel of these days.
Give us true hearts and tender,
  And plain, old-fashioned ways!
Of men like Allen Thurman
  This world will never cloy,
Who calls his old wife "Sweetheart,"
  And loves her like a boy!

A Word of Advice.

DO you know a luscious mouth,
Honey oozing like the South ?
Lips like bashful roses red
On a bed of lilies wed ?
        Do not think about it.
Thinking leads to mad desire
That will scorch the heart like fire :
If a sweet mouth haunts you still,
Put it from you with a will.
        Never think about it.

Do you know a pair of eyes,
Dreamy soft and passion-wise ?
Or mayhap a pair you've seen
Of serene and haughty sheen.
        Do not think about 'em.
Liquid eyes are like a pool
Where one looks and sees a fool.
Can you deem that such are kind
If they kill your peace of mind ?
        Never think about 'em.

Do you know a downy cheek,
Peachy-plump and satin-sleek,
Where, when laughter's zephyrs sweep,
Dimples deep like eddies keep ?
        Do not think about it.
Dimples come and dimples go
Where the roses stain the snow,
But the wound that did the harm

E'en outlives the fatal charm.
Never think about it.

'Tis a rule for young and old,
Good to keep and good to hold :
Woman's charms are devil's bait —
All too late we mourn our fate.
Do not think about 'em.
Lily hands and fairy feet,
Luscious lips and glances sweet —
Love's a chain, and these are links ;
He's a slave who looks and thinks.
Never think about 'em.

Dandelions.

ALL among the green grass
The dandelions grow ;
Yellow dandelions,
Pretty dandelions !
Let the babies pick them,
Toddling to and fro.
When I hear the children
Shouting in the grass,
When I see a dandelion,
Though but one it be,
All my days of manhood
Like a vision pass,
And my baby sweetheart
Plays again with me !

All among the tall grass
The dandelions nod ;
    Yellow dandelions,
    Stately dandelions !
Let the children pick them,
Romping on the sod ;
Roses of the poor folk,
Springing everywhere.
When a single dandelion
Now I chance to see,
Comes a dream of boyhood,
With its vision fair,
And my school-girl sweetheart
Laughs and kisses me !

All among the lush grass
The dandelions sway ;
    Fluffy dandelions,
    Ghosts of dandelions !
Let the summer breezes
Blow them all away,
Like the joys that scatter
In our early years.
When I see a dandelion
Ghost upon the lea,
All my past arises,
And I think, with tears,
How my little sweetheart
Sleeps and dreams of me !

The Last Sweetheart.

GRAN'PA'S locks are white as snow,
  Those he still possesses,
Ghosts of curls of long ago,
  Wraiths of boyhood's tresses.
    Wrinkles o'er his features thin
      Zigzag without pity, ·
    Like the streets and alleys in
      Famous Boston city.

Time has bent his form with years,
  And his legs are thinner
And less comely than the shears
  Used by any tinner.
    Lusty was he once and gay,
      Full of manhood's graces;
    But of that long vanished day
      There are now few traces.

Yet he in his youthful pride
  Pleased the fair sex greatly;
Many lassies for him sighed,—
  Many ladies stately.
    Hearts once throbbed and ached for him;
      Tears wet silken lashes;
    But those eyes in death are dim,
      And those hearts are ashes.

Gran'pa has one sweetheart yet,
  Daintiest of creatures,
Whose two eyes of deepest jet
  Still approve his features.

Nellie is her name, you see,
And, if I remember
What her age is, she was three
Some time last December.

Oft her hands, so chubby fair,
O'er his face she passes
Tenderly, and with great care
Not to touch his glasses.
  Oft his form I've seen her scan,
  And I've caught her saying:
  "Gran'pa's such a handsome man,"
  Thus her love betraying.

Little Susie Lilly.

L ITTLE Susie Lilly,
  Strolling down Broadway,
Wonders at the windows
  Decked for Christmas Day.
Here and there she lingers,
  Dreaming all the time
What she'd buy for Christmas,
  If she had a dime.

Little Susie Lilly
  Never has a cent;
All her father's money
  Goes to pay the rent;
All her mother's earnings
  Go for beer and bread.
Susie thinks a girl is
  Lucky when she's fed.

Little Susie Lilly,
  Strolling down the street,
Hasn't decent shoes to
  Hide her chubby feet ;
Hasn't e'en a single
  Dress that's fit to wear,
And of gloves or mittens
  Never had a pair !

Little Susie Lilly
  Is so poorly clad,
Don't you think a dress would
  Make her very glad ?
Don't you think if she were
  Told to go and choose,
She would pick a jacket
  Or a pair of shoes ?

Little Susie Lilly,
  Standing in the snow,
What is in the window
  That has charmed you so ?
Is it shoes or mittens ?
  Is it cakes or pies ?
Bless me, it's a dolly
  That can wink its eyes !

Old Things are Best.

OLD things are best.   We wander
  So strangely and so lonely
From here to that world yonder.
Why not grow fond and fonder
  In tried affections only ?

Old friends are best. Their faces
Each year seem dearer, dearer,
And glow with new-found graces;
Then, ah! These vacant places
    But bring the living nearer.

Old homes are best. The laughter
That tells of childhood's pleasures
Beneath the ancient rafter,
Surpasses all that's after,
    And all of manhood's treasures.

Old love is best. Its sweetness
Makes pleasant Sorrow's chalice;
And, spite of Time's dread fleetness,
It gains in calm completeness
    And laughs at Age's malice.

Old faith is best: the teaching
Of heart-enshrined mothers.
What profits subtle preaching,
Or blind and eager reaching
    For doubt that mocks and smothers?

Old ways are best: the gladness
Of simpler lives and fitter,
Ere wealth had come with madness,
Or folly left its sadness,
    And sin its lessons bitter.

Old things are best. The glimmer
Of age forbids new choices.
Oh, as mine eyes grow dimmer,
Faintly across the shimmer
    Waft me the old, sweet voices!

A Letter from Ireland.

I'VE a letter from Erin this bright Christmas day,
  Which my old mother sends to me over the sea;
'Tis a message of love from the friends far away,
  A gift of all others most welcome to me.
Wonder not at my tears, for these pages were penned
  In the cot where, a baby, I rolled on the floor,
And what dearer token than this could she send —
  This sprig of green shamrock from old Erin's shore?

" Merry Christmas," she writes, "to the boy of my
      pride,
  And I hope this will reach him at no other time.
Oh, the oceans are deep and the oceans are wide,
  And the mountains between us are rugged to climb,
But a mother's affection is wide as the earth,
  And lasts till the heart that it thrills is no more;
So I send you my love from the home of your birth
  And a sprig of green shamrock from old Erin's
      shore."

Dear old Irish mother, so tender and kind!
  I'll be true to my God, to myself and to you.
And what lack of manhood or grace can you find
  When a boy to his mother is faithful and true?
Yes, I'll wear in my bosom this letter of mine;
  I will treasure this gift from the land I adore,
For the heart of a mother is love's purest shrine,
  And the shamrock grows fairest in Erin Asthore!

Songs of the Soul.

The Agnostic's Creed.

FROM whence I come, or whither go,
My creed is this : I do not know.
Into this creed all others flow.

I am a flickering spark of mind;
Vast darkness is before, behind —
Darkness to me, for I am blind.

Lo, in a blade of grass there dwell
Dread mysteries I cannot spell,
Higher than heaven, deeper than hell.

Things were, and are, and are to be ;
I peer not into mystery,
And cry, made bold through fear, "I see."

Things were, and are, and go their way,
Whether they govern or obey ;
With them I go and cannot stray.

"I do not know." All thought sublime,
All prophesies of former time,
But hide this pearl in seas of slime.

And I, who neither fear nor trust,
Holding this creed because I must,
Shall not be mocked, alive or dust.

Immortality.

WHATE'ER begins must end.   So say
    Philosophers both old and new;
And nature's round—birth, fruit, decay—
    Doth prove the adage true.

Snug in the unripe acorn's coat
    A fallen oak tree slumbereth;
The new-born infant's lusty throat
    Must rattle soon in death.

And so, whatever hath no end
    Never began and ne'er was born;
Its origin and finish blend
    As night fades into morn.

Infinity was by a ring
    In former ages signed and taught;
Surely a plain and simple thing,
    Yet food for grandest thought.

God is the end and final cause,
    The Alpha and Omega He,
Before beginnings, more than laws,
    He was and is to be.

And if our souls are plumed to flit
    Through being's circle, near and far,
They lived before the sun was lit
    Or heaven had a star.

Oh, listen, Brothers, listen well!
    It were a cheerful thing to hear

An angel harp or shriek from hell
    To rid us from this fear.

For we are brutes or prisoned gods;
    And there is none of us can guess
What life we passed before these clods,
    This vile forgetfulness.

The Three Still Voices.

EGO.

HOW lie the dead below?
    Above them grasses grow;
Willow and cypress weep along their streets;
    Patient, within each tomb,
    Vainly they wait for doom;
It glads not them if time or creeps or fleets.

    They neither sleep nor dream;
    They neither are nor seem;
They are not now, and yet forevermore.
    Our minds, like rats or moles,
    Can dig into their holes,
And watch them lose the likeness which they bore.

    On dewy dawns of spring
    Glad larks above them sing;
Long summer days brood o'er them, soft and kind;
    In every winter night
    Their slabs gleam weird and white,
And snows drift round them on the drifting wind.

Storms come with phantom hosts,
Moaning like damned ghosts—
Like ghosts far off and sad with all despair ;
And fiends, that shriek aloud,
Rend the dead winter's shroud,
And flutter it in wanton frenzy there.

What are the names they knew ?
Some plainly writ, 'tis true—
Their owners died at such a recent date.
Old Time walks here, alone,
And rubs them from each stone,
As children rub the letters from a slate.

And what is fame to those
O'er whom deep Lethe flows,
Who know not of men's curses or their tears ?
Our voices fade in air;
They hear not, lying there,
The thunder of the treading of the years.

Armies above them shout
In victory or rout ;
Great cannon boom and shiver overhead ;
Old creeds to earth are hurled,
Thrones fall and shake the world—
All this the dead know not, for they are dead.

Be wise, Myself, be wise ;
Live life then, ere it flies ;
Oh, be not cheated by a lying creed :
Sate well each eager sense,
Or else thou wilt go hence,
And, having died, thou wilt be dead indeed.

ALTER EGO.

How shall a man shut out
His foolish hope, his doubt?
Such wondrous overtones about him ring.
So oft, when wine is best,
There comes a vague unrest,
A chill, as though from unseen angel wing.

Why do we love to flee
From scenes of revelry
Alone to wander 'neath the awful stars?
To gaze into the deeps
Till something in us leaps
And fiercely seems to shake its prison bars?

To stand upon the beach
And let our dim eyes reach
Beyond the light-house and far out amain;
To list the rhythmic roar
Of waves that march ashore,
And hear them chant in deep, prophetic strain?

Who knows what far, fair isles,
Where summer dreams and smiles,
What slopes they saw all sweet with lotos' blows?
What shores of peace and bliss
They fled from with a kiss
Before they hither came — who knows, who knows?

And if old Triton rise,
Dim seen where sea-scud flies,
Floating serene through foamy trough and swell,

How doth it lift and thrill
To hear him softly shrill,
Then shriek and thunder on his hollow shell.

Thus stars and storms and seas
Hint at great mysteries,
And link the man to worthiness and power,
Showing the simple mind
What sages often find
In vernal sprout or modest hedgerow flower.

Ah me, in wretched way!
Blind at the full of day,
Having no wings, yet sick for love of flight;
Warmed by celestial fire,
Enwrapped in base desire,
Hoping for morn and cowering in the night.

JUSTICE.

Delve not for hidden things;
Drink from Truth's wayside springs,
And grovel not because the fleet years flee.
Good surely is man's best,
For this must be God's test:
"Not what he was, but what he strove to be."

Our Two Lives.

I HOLD with those philosophers who claim
   That mind is all in all;
'Tis thought that feeds the sun's undying flame,
   And shapes this earthly ball.

You are no dwelling-place of flesh, wherein
    There hides a form of fear ;
Your face no mask is for a face whose grin
    Mocks ever all things dear.

You think you live ; but soon you die and rot ;
    Your features tremble to a blur,
And then, anon, your very name's forgot,
    And lo ! you never were.

We live two lives thus : one in which there beams
    By turns a sun and moon ;
The other while we range the realm of dreams,
    Wearing its magic shoon.

Wild songs, low sobs, faint echoings often drift
    From that life into this,
And sometimes greet us, peeping through a rift,
    Faces of those we miss.

But who our unremembered dreams can guess?
    Can any poet tell
What poppied meads with eager feet we press,
    What fields of asphodel ?

Nay, this our madness, that we think is life,
    Lasts only for a day,
And then we leave its folly and its strife
    To sleep and dream for aye.

On Finding a Beautiful Moth.

DOUBT and I, one summer day,
   Through green wood and meadow gay
Chanced in random mood to stray.

God was in the brooding air,
Round about us everywhere,
Thrilling, shaping all things fair.

But the will and way divine
Were too subtile, deep and fine
For those careless eyes of mine.

Far about us then, as still,
Woven threads of matchless will,
Twirled the stars with awful skill.

But I stood owl-eyed at gaze,
Blinded by the noontide blaze,
Witless of the stellar maze.

Marvel not to hear that I
Learned of matters deep and high
From a gorgeous butterfly.

"Sure," I said, "some master mind
Such a dainty shape designed —
All these hues arranged, combined."

Doubt was silent. "Yes," I said,
"'Twas an artist's hand that led
These fine lines, these colors spread.

" He was one that dipped his brush
 In the dawntime's virgin blush,
 In the gray of twilight's hush.

" Here are tints that die or swoon,
 Gold of sun and gold of moon,
 White of winter, green of June.

" This symmetric, dainty thing,
 This divine imagining,
 Chance ne'er fashioned." — Doubt took wing.

So it ofttimes haps, I wis,
 They whose eyes the great sea miss
 Hear the shoreward breakers hiss.

God has writ our rightful creed
 Both for wise and simple need ; —
 Even they who run may read.

A Mystery.

OUR baby boy one day'
 Folded his violet eyes,
And from his waxen clay
His white soul flew away
 To far-off Paradise.

His little hands so fair
 We crossed upon his breast,
And standing by him there
We gave him to the care
 Of One who doeth best.

And when to final sleep
　　We laid him soft and low,
We could not help but heap
Upon him lilies deep
　　And roses pure as snow.

And then, with courage great,
　　His mother faced the years;
But oft, when it was late,
Among his toys she sate
　　And fondled them with tears.

But now another child,
　　With wondrous violet eyes,
Rests on her bosom mild,
And smiles as he had smiled,
　　To-day in Paradise.

And something seems to say
　　To her, so sad before:
"The soul that flew away
Is back again to-day;
　　Sweet mother, weep no more!"

Higher.

HIGHER!
　　This shall my watchword be,
And this one thought my soul inspire,
For I am keen and free.

　　Higher!
Yea, even in defeat
Hold I my lofty purpose higher
And deem it still more sweet.

Higher !
Though Victory should smile
And, bringing me my one desire,
   Should say : " Rest thee awhile."

Higher !
This be my shibboleth
Of those few friends whom I require
   And love in life and death.

Higher !
Up to that frigid height
Where clinging needs and lusts expire
   And thought flies strong and light.

Higher !
God, save me from old age,
From listlessness and eyes that tire
   Of Thine illumined page !

Higher !
Oh, let this spark divine
Leap glittering to the central fire,
   The all-pervading shine.

Brothers.

SPIDER,
   At my window spinning,
Weaving circles wider, wider,
   From the deft beginning ;

Running
Rings and spokes, until you
Build your silken death-trap cunning, —
   Shall I catch you — kill you ?

Sprawling,
Nimble, shrewd as Circe ;
Death's your only aim and calling.
Why should you have mercy ?

Strike thee ?
Not for rapine willful.
Man himself is too much like thee,
Only not so skillful.

Rife in
Thee lives our Creator.
Thou'rt a shape to hold a life in —
I am nothing greater.

On a Cat Mummy.

PREPOSTEROUS cat, from Egypt's soil arisen,
  Where thou hast lain beneath the sand seas flat,
The countless years had power thy face to wizen,
  But not to wreck, for thou art still a cat.

I will not point at thee with jesting finger,
  Nor pass thee by as though unworthy thought,
For there is much in thee to make me linger ;
  Those sightless eyes are with high meaning fraught.

'Tis hard indeed for modern thought or notion
  To move along on ancient Koptic line,
Or hold, by any sort of weird devotion,
  Grimalkin clothed in attributes divine.

We upstarts have a curious way of linking
  Puss with old dames and flights upon a broom,

But Egypt's reverential mode of thinking
  Ere Homer's day ran back to earlier gloom.

How very modern is our prophet Moses!
  Our Christ himself but theme for recent talk,
While we are few when counted with the noses
  That owned the sway of Horus and of hawk.

Five thousand years! The brain grows sick and dizzy.
  But long ere then Phtah ruled beside the Nile,
And swarming millions, brown and blithe and busy,
  Throve in the dreamy splendor of his smile.

Most ancient cat! When thou were swathed and twisted ·
  In costly shroud and laid in sacred grave,
Apis and Pharaoh vainly were resisted,
  And gentle Isis deigned to bless and save.

Those gods are dead, and faded is their splendor ;
  Their countless years are but a day that's done,
While Bethlehem's star, with radiance pure and tender,
  Outshines in glory Egypt's fiercest sun.

The granite statue of sublime Rameses
  On Memphis plain stands desolate to-day,
And years drift by, like summer's cloudy fleeces,
  Forever changing and the same for aye.

Broad lotus leaves still on Nile's bosom quiver,
  Still lives the Sphinx in many a Koptic face,
But never Pharaoh drifts across the river
  In golden boat to his long resting-place.

O wondrous cat! Time leveled many a city,
  Pantheons fell, great nations were forgot,

But thou wast hid, and now, in scorn and pity,
  Comest to taunt me with my fleeting lot.

Out of my sight! I will no more abide thee.
  Thy weird grotesqueness makes me chill and faint;
Thou art too hoar; I cannot well deride thee,
  But I will spurn thee ere I suffer taint.

Curse on those old Egyptians and their science!
  Types live, and change doth keep this old world sweet.
We pass and come again: why bid defiance
  To Nature, and be spurned beneath her feet?

Voices of nature join in ceaseless pæan!
  Death is but change and joyful motherhood;
And through the chorus whisper, Galilean,
  "Why live at all except for doing good?"

Oh, Motherless Child!

THIS is the house; the shutters
    Are closed as ne'er before,
And that is crape which flutters
    Beside the open door.
And there, within the garden
    Her baby boy sits piling
A heap of gathered pebbles.
    Look, friend, the babe is smiling—
        Oh, motherless child!

Nay, call him not; hereafter
    His grief with years will grow.
Check not his infant laughter;
    He is too young to know.

Too young, or smiles he wisely,
    Feeling a gentle spirit,
Whom our dim eyes can see not,
    Is at his side or near it?
            Oh, motherless child!

Come, friend, our kindly weeping
    Can bring them no relief;
I would not view her sleeping,
    Nor see her loved one's grief.
I fear the scene would haunt me
    In all my future straying.
The white form in the parlor,
    The little boy a-playing —
            Oh, motherless child!

But why is death intruding
    Upon us with such fear?
Is not the Christ-love brooding
    Above, and watching near?
My soul, too weak and simple
    To cope with doubt and error,
Hast found thyself forsaken?
    Dost cry in sudden terror,
            Oh, motherless child?

Laura Bridgman.

WHAT think you were the joys of that freed being
    When first there broke upon her new-oped vision,
With purple clouds about them dimly fleeing,
    The far-off turrets of her home elysian?

When first she heard, distrait with bliss and wonder,
   The music of the spheres about her ringing,
Afar and near their golden hum and thunder,
   And all the morning stars together singing?

How many years she dwelt in prison, waiting!
   No ray of sun relieved the darkness bitter,
And no stray bird around her window grating
   Flew now and then with friendly song and twitter.

Her prison was like ours—a little dimmer:
   We stumble, grope and listen; all our peering
Is by chance rays and through a sifting glimmer;
   Confused and wrong is our most perfect hearing.

O, Jailer Death! thy terrors have been sounded
   Long in men's hearts and much in song and story;
Yet, since we are by light and love surrounded,
   We dread thee not.   Let in the waiting glory!

Singing all the Way.

IN the farmhouse door grandmother stands
   With lovelit face and outstretched hands,
While up the road with flying feet
Comes little Marjie, flushed and sweet;
In through the gate she trips so gay,
Singing all the way, singing all the way.

"Gran'ma," she cries, "I never missed
One word in all the spelling list.
To-morrow I'll be at the head,

An' teacher praised me when I read ;
So I came home from school to-day
Singing all the way, singing all the way."

Grandmother kissed the little one,
Then wistful watched the sinking sun,
Where, back of clouds and changing skies,
A wondrous city seemed to rise.
She's always glad, that woman gray —
Singing all the way, singing all the way.

" The Invisible."

THE red men, whom we so despise,
And proudly try to civilize,
Are wiser in some ways by far
Than we and all our teachers are.

We preach the after-life, and range
Through Nature's round of ceaseless change,
And search the hopes and fears of men,
To prove that we shall live again.

We only half believe, at best ;
Our faith stands not the greatest test :
For when our friends depart we weep
More than for those who do but sleep.

And on each marble slab we write
Some legend of the spirit's flight,
Lest, passing by, we might forget
That he who died is living yet,

The Indian, with a single phrase,
The ghost of doubt and terror lays,
And lifts the viewless curtain spread
Between us and the so-called dead.

He knows no "dead": just for a space
His friends have faded, form and face.
Through Nature's strong and subtle spell
They have become "invisible."

We are too fine and wise.   We need
Much less of logic and of creed.
Oh, let the untaught forest-child
Teach us his credence undefiled !

Let us no longer say "Our Dead,"
Nor think that those we love have fled.
They are "Invisible," as we
Shall close our eyes some day, and see.

Unmasked.

AFTER long years apart,
    Two old friends met by chance ;
Each knew, with quickened heart,
    The other at a glance.

After a fleeting day
    Two souls met, face to face ;
Each looked, and, muttering "Nay !"
    Fled past through windless space.

Trinity Church-yard.

THERE in the midst of the city,
  Bounded by turbulent streets,
Rivers of strife and of passion,
Lieth the acre of God.

There in the ocean of frenzy,
Safe from the wrath of its waves,
Quiet for years and forever
Resteth the Island of Peace.

Out from the portals of heaven
Shineth a beautiful light,
Gilding its mountains with splendor,
Flooding its hollows with love.

Gayly the slumberous poppy
Bloometh o'er valley and slope,
And by each dwelling-place windeth
Lethe, soft-rippling and deep.

God save the soul in the waters,
Clinging to hope like a spar,
Longing to rest on the island
In its ineffable hush !

Once on a magical Sabbath,
Wandering there in the morn,
Learned I a wonderful lesson,
Simple, yet greater than speech.

There, on a moss-covered marble,
Liveth the name of a babe,

Laid in the cradle of Nature
Years twice a hundred ago.

Grieve for it not, O ye mothers!
She that mourned longest is dead ;
Lives that are ended are equal,
All of them equal and naught.

Heartaches and sorrows and troubles,
Are they not weeds of a day,
Sown in the dust of our bodies,
Having no roots in the soul ?

This was the question I pondered,
When, like an answer from God,
Suddenly thundered above me
All of old Trinity's bells.

Chant yet again, brazen singers!
Chant till the measureless sky,
Yea, and the dust of the church-yard
Tremble to glorious chimes.

Moods.

Longing for Rain.

FOR weary months the earth has waited, longing,
  Till waiting grows almost a steady pain,
And memories to the thirsty soul come thronging
  Of eastern fields made green by summer rain.

A Reminiscence.

O JOY intense! of scenting and of feeling,
  With panting birds, droop-winged in sultry shade.
A sudden freshness on the senses stealing,
  A sweet relief the quivering air invade.

  Falls a big drop, smooth and plump
  In the dust with sudden "thump."
  Others with increasing patter
  On the shingles rap and splatter.

    Plowboy, whistling at the plow;
    Lover, with half-finished vow;
    Sage, intent on mighty theme;
    Dreamer, roaming in a dream—
        Run for shelter
        Helter skelter!

Now the rain is pouring down,
Sparing neither sage nor clown.
                Now the air is
                Full of fairies.

Hear the still increasing rattle
Of the lively mimic battle.
To and fro upon the roof
Gallops many a well-shod hoof.
As the noisy fray he leaves
How each fleeing pigmy grieves,
In the bubble and the gurgle of the eaves!

    Hark! a lively snatch is chanted
    By the robbin, no whit daunted.
    Ere the eaves have ceased from spouting
    You may hear his sweet, wild shouting;
You may often hear him calling
Even while the rain is falling,
Ringing high his note of glee,
Simple, hearty, clear and free:
    "Sunshine will come again
        When the rain is over;
    Honey bees will hum again
    In the wet, red clover!"

Rain at Last.

DOWN rocky chasm, wide and deep,
    Whose bed was dry through summer days,
With many a run, and many a leap,
    A noisy, foam-flecked brooklet strays.

Soon will a river's widening floods,
   Mad with the burst of long pent rains,
Come thundering from the mountain woods
   To dash in fury on the plains.

Soon will the hill-top and the cloud
   Send forth their cataracts far and near,
And voice of many waters loud
   Will all the caverned summits hear.

Thus oft do mountain tribes, grown strong,
   With hearts too big for bounds of yore,
Down all the rocky passes throng,
   And on the frightened valleys pour.

O people of the plains, build high,
   Build strong your battlements, build tight,
Before the angry floods come nigh
   And sack your city in the night!

Rain in the Mountains.

'TIS winter where Sierra's peaks gigantic
   Loom in eternal phalanx by the West,
And now the mist, in folds and loopings antic,
   Hangs drapery round each grim and ancient crest.

What scenes of vastness and of grandeur varied,
   Impressive sounds and overwhelming sights,
Dwell round these cliffs, rain-plowed and lightning-
     quarried,
   These lonely aisles and earthquake-builded heights!

On him who wanders here, with what intensity
Do feelings of man's nothingness intrude ;
How is he swallowed up in the immensity
Of nature in her wild and stormful mood !

Long ere the Genoese set sail, exploring,
With ships inverted, far in unknown tides,
Forgotten men have yearly heard the roaring
Of new-born torrents on these mountain-sides.

These stately peaks, unseen of eyes Caucasian,
From time's daybreak have reared their heads on
high ;
'Mid shifting years of untold peace and passion,
Have watched the pigmy ages shrink and die.

Grim monuments of long forgotten races !
Crush not my spirit 'neath your piles sublime ;
Let not the legend on your battered faces
Too much oppress the fleeting son of Time.

O man, look up, and tell these giants hoary
That greatness is not all a thing of size ;
Thou art a spark of that Celestial Glory
Whose wisdom set their heads among the skies.

Rain in the Heart.

NO flashing snows and crystal air,
That send the warm blood dancing free ;
No jingling bells and mingled glee,
And gay steeds dashing here and there.

But days of damp and gloom and chill,
  Till thought dwells only on such theme
  As faces that are but a dream,
And voices now forever still.

From o'er the blue Sierra's peaks,
  Across the great plains, wild and wide,
  Across the Mississippi's tide,
There comes a voice that sadly speaks.

He dwelt within my soul, and read
  The secrets graven on my heart;
  Of all my life he was a part,
Yet now, afar, he lieth dead.

His were the gifts we strive to share:
  Discretion far beyond his years;
  Wit that would flash a smile through tears,
And span their rainbow on despair.

Some things I never knew.   God grant
  He called that priceless gem his own,
  Without possessing which, alone,
All other things are utter want.

Again I see those college days;
  We sit in some familiar room,
  Whiling away the coming gloom,
And on the misty future gaze.

Anon the lamp shines from the desk,
  When from the well-filled shelf is brought
  Some legacy of ancient thought,
Dwelling in characters grotesque.

And often, when the path was blind,
  With skillful step the way he led,
  And conjured up the mighty Dead,
Communing with them, mind to mind.

These things belong to days of yore;
  And now I listen, all aghast,
  While still from out the darkness vast
There comes a voice that cries: "No more."

No more; and yet, through all the years,
  My heart shall have a place for thee,
  Where sweetest flowers of Memory
Shall grow, bedewed by frequent tears.

The Talkative Wife.

(A poor companion for the rainy season.)

OLD Solomon hinted, and he ought to know,
    That a woman of quarrelsome mind,
Like the dropping one hears when the skies overflow,
Never ceases, no matter how weary you grow,
    And is harder to squelch than the wind.

There once was a woman who talked, talked, talked,
    And she was a serious ill;
For, whether she rode or whether she walked,
She couldn't be stopped, and she wouldn't be balked;
    She really never was still.

At morning, at noon, and all through the day,
    She kept up her horrible din;

She chattered and scolded and gossiped away,
And talked even when she had nothing to say —
　　But that's not an uncommon sin.

Her husband, of all men, had most cause to weep
　　(She had one, I'm sorry to tell),
For all through the night she would chattering keep,
Kind angels defend us! she talked in her sleep,
　　And his bed was a foretaste of hell.

But all earthly doings must finally cease;
　　Time's prowess were vainly denied;
So this woman's tongue did at last find release,
For she lay down one night and for once held her peace —
　　'Twas the night that she lay down and died.

And now we are come to a strange anecdote,
　　But the truth must be told, come what may;
She chanced to be talking when Death seized her throat,
And though she ne'er afterward uttered a note,
　　Her jaw still kept wagging away.

They tied close her mouth with a napkin and strap,
　　But such force had the muscles acquired
That her jaws flew apart with a forcible snap,
Then together again like the jaws of a trap,
　　And then worked as though ne'er to be tired.

Years after, three doctors this strange story knew,
　　And agreed that the bones must arise
(A decision that doctors are pained to come to,
But if their devotion to science is true,
　　Their feelings they oft sacrifice).

So they called upon madam, and found her within,
  But the sight brought their blood to a chill,
For her face upward leered with a skeleton grin,
And, most horrid of all, may I never more sin
  If the jaw was not working on still!

So the doctors agreed, and I think were not wrong,
  As soon as their heads became level,
That the will of a woman is wonderful strong,
And works over spaces and intervals long,
  And defies even Death and the Devil!

Alone Together.

(How rainy days might be pleasant.)

CLING closer love, and press your dear,
  Soft cheek to mine, and feel no fear,
  Though ghostly winds without complain,
  And scared drops fly against the pane;
For you are here and I am here,

And storms will vent their spite in vain,
If love look forth in sweet disdain,
  And thou, within the firelight's cheer,
    Cling closer, love.

More bitter storms of grief and pain
In after years will vex us twain.
  Ah, then, in light of love sincere,
  Come near my sweet, and still more near—
Ever, in time of life's dark rain,
    Cling closer, love.

Two Moods.

THE pine tree at my window drips
From all its slender finger tips;
The wild wind sobs with pale, thin lips.

What awful wailings do I hear,
Unutterably faint and drear ?
Ah me, the wind tells not such fear !

Long with this dreadful thought I've striven :
Is not my heart distraught and riven
By shrieks of souls, fiend-scourged and driven ?

Can I not see their robes of gray
Trailing athwart the somber day,
As in some nightmare by Doré?

Alas ! why will that laggard stand,
And shake the sash with viewless hand ?
Away ! and join yon fleeing band.

I do not dare mine eyes to strain
Lest they should see against the pane
Some ghastly face, bedrenched with rain.

There in the old hearth on its bed
The great oak log is lying dead :
No flame elfs dance at foot or head.

I am alone to-day, alone ;
Behind lies many a sad milestone,
And many a sterile field, wind-sown.

I kissed my love one starry dawn,
And turned away my face, pain-drawn,
Knowing she could not follow on.

"I am alone to-day," I said,
"For love and grief in me are wed,
And she — she is not even dead."

My friend said : "Let me go with you;
Tho' woman fail, will I be true."
Alas ! my way he little knew.

And thus, unknown of all mankind,
With thin, wan face 'gainst rain and wind,
I go right on, nor look behind.

Hath not my noviceship sufficed ?
Ah, I have suffered like the Christ !
And smiled as though by joy enticed.

Yea, like the damned have I despaired,
And none have asked me how I fared,
Because they neither knew nor cared.

By graves of mine I've stood at night,
To ponder o'er the sleepers' plight,
While winter spread their couches white.

And oft, when spring her revels kept,
Have I within their city wept,
Because they, only, slept and slept.

And joy has seized me, such as fills
The robin's heart, and overspills,
Or is in dancing daffodils.

And I have lain in shady swoon
Throughout a summer's afternoon,
And heard the turtle coo and croon.

Full oft a million honey bees'
Æolian harps in bloomy trees
Have lulled my soul to sweetest ease.

Oft have I strayed on wild sea strands
To watch old Neptune wave his hands,
And hear him call his plumed bands.

Nature's whole diapase I know,
From fall of leaves on crusted snow
To thunder music, high or low.

Children are cherubs in my eyes ;
Their happy voices seem to rise
From out a long lost paradise.

My heart bleeds for the world's forlorn,
And looketh ever toward the morn
When no man shall his brother scorn.

And I would liefer sing one song
To free a slave or right a wrong
Than be chief fool to fashion's throng.

Ah ! what is this ? The fire once more
Is burning with a merry roar ;
The chill is gone, the gloom is o'er.

And see, the clouds are fleeing far
Before the sun's keen scimitar.
How bright the pine tree's jewels are!

Why should a poet thirst for praise ?
The sun shines bright on cloudiest days,
The linnet sings by loneliest ways.

The Unexpected.

(Sudden Sunshine.)

WHEN clouds are black, and rain has long been
        chilling,
   The sudden sun will ofttimes struggle through,
Anon with splendor all the prospect filling,
   From jeweled trees to skies of deepest blue.

When lives are dark, and hope has ceased beguiling,
   Some unexpected gleam may glad the sight,
And after years, in fortune's perfect smiling,
   Be filled with naught save honor, love and light.

Fugitive Verse.

Walt Whitman.

A N old man once saw I,
 Bowed low was he with time,
 Heart-frosted, white with rime,
Ready and ripe to die.

Upon a cliff he stood,
 Above the sea's unrest;
 His beard broke on his breast
In venerable flood.

And suddenly there came
 From far, with airy tread,
 A maiden, round whose head
There burned a wreath of flame.

Ah God, but she was fair!
 To look were to disdain
 All other joy and pain,
And love her to despair.

"I come," she cried, in tone
 Like sweetest siren song;
 "Though I have tarried long,
I come, my own — my own!

"See, Love, 'tis love compels
  These kisses, priceless, rare;
  Come, let me crown thy hair
With wreathed immortelles."

The old man answered her—
  His voice was like the sea:
  "Comest to mock at me?
Mine eyes are all ablur.

"Thou art too late. In sooth,
  Naught earthly makes me glad.
  Where wert thou in my mad,
My eager, fiery youth?"

"Nay, grieve not thou," she said,
  "For I have loved full oft,
  And at my lovers scoffed,
Alive, to woo them dead."

"O fiend," I cried, "for shame!"
  Yielding to wrath's surprise.
  She turned. I knew the eyes
And siren face of Fame.

𝔓an.

THAT old god Pan,
  By some sweet stream that ran,
Through dreamy fields Arcadian,

Safe hid would lie
'Mongst reeds and rushes high,
And watch the flashing waves go by.

Often he made
Soft music in the shade,
And all things listened while he played.

He earliest knew
What sound souls fair and true
In whispering reeds imprisoned grew.

'Twas he that in
Their hollow pipes and thin
Found all of nature's dulcet din.

He played; the thrush,
Hid in leaf-bower lush,
With head awry, grew mute and hush,

And honey bees,
Quiring in blossomed trees,
Would cease to list his melodies.

His pipe to hear,
The timid fawn stole near,
And, quite entranced, forgot its fear.

And many a face
Of nymph and woodland grace
Peeped through into his hiding-place.

Bards of to-day,
On scrannel pipes that play,
Your discords fill us with dismay.

Oh, that some man
By stream Arcadian
Might find the Syrinx of old Pan!

Music.

SNUG in the nest the young bird lies
 Until its wings are strong,
And then it cleaves the buoyant skies,
Bearing, if near or far it flies,
 A message and a song.

So fledging thoughts, unfinished things,
 Nest in the poet's head ;
But Music trains their sprouting wings
Till from the poet's brain each springs,
 And flies when he is dead !

Robert Herrick.

1591-1674.

DELICIOUS May is with us now,
 Bud days, and days of tryst and vow ;
And is not this the time of times
To read dear Bobby Herrick's rhymes ?

Sweet singer, dumb these many years,
What is it thus thy verse endears ?
Each spring the flowers bloom anew,
Each spring thy rhymes—they're flowers too.

In Devonshire's fair fields of green
The primrose yet is thickly seen,
And daffodils still haste away
As soon, alas ! as in thy day.

We pass, ere noon, and are forgot;
But thy sweet voice, why heed it not,
Allowing us, in gentlest rhyme,
The harmless folly of our time?

Soon must all things that glad the sight
Be drowned with us in endless night.
Ah! happy man, who chanced to say:
"Gather ye rosebuds while ye may."

E'en rare Ben Jonson's fame is half
Due to his curious epitaph;
But thou shalt 'scape oblivion's doom
While springs shall smile and flowers bloom.

The Organ-grinder.

ABOVE the quiet village street,
   Cool willow branches wave and meet,
And locust blossoms fall in sweet
Midsummer snow beneath the feet.

Often adown the dusty way
Sleek cattle indolently stray;
And groups of little children play
In sun and shadow all the day.

Sometimes an organ-grinder brown
Comes with his wrinkled simian clown,
And sets his tuneful burden down
Before the finest house in town.

Then soon a merry band and fair,
Entranced, applaud each hackneyed air,
Or shout at Jocko's antics there,
As at some mime of genius rare.

And I, though I should list my fill,
To some old maëstro's magic skill,
Could never feel such honest thrill
As these young alchemists of ill.

He goes, as organ-grinders do,
To play elsewhere his tunes anew;
The laughter of that merry crew
Dies down the leafy avenue.

They follow him in Fairyland,
A region where all winds are bland,
Where every hour is pleasure planned,
And wonders lie on every hand.

Pied Piper of our village street,
Play on, thy wheezy tunes repeat!
Once more to think such music sweet
I'd toss a fortune at thy feet!

To Walt Whitman.

(On receiving his book.)

I THANK thee, Good Gray Poet, for thy book;
　How much I prize it thou couldst only know
By knowing all the love I feel for thee,
And this is partly why: The land is full
Of wights who live by rhyme. They prate of art,
And, having no great message to the race,

Fill all the public prints with pretty verse.
Mere twittering sparrows they, that flit around
The sacred summit of old Helicon.
Sore sick of these, I ope thy book, and lo !
The twitterings cease and in their stead I hear
The voice of ancient forests and the seas,
That "first and last confession of the globe."
Perhaps with thee I mourn the "unnam'd dead,"
And in my heart set up a monument
To all the heroes that have fought and failed.
And ever as I read, hope grows in me,
Hope like a bird that sings as cheerily
Amid a dreary waste of arctic snows
As though lush summer smiled and earth were gay.
Full oft I dream of mighty destinies
That wait our country, and I see her sons,
Her fierce athletic daughters and her sons,
The matchless hosts of perfect years to be,
Winning great victories in the fields of peace.
So this thy book is such a prize to me
As if a sailor, far inland, should find
A shell within whose tinted chambers dwelt
Old Neptune's grizzled wraith.   What joy were his
To put its cool lips to his ear and list
The crooning moan and whistle of the sea !

Death of the Stag.

A STATELY stag comes down to drink
Beside the mountain lakelet's brink ;
Around him, towering to the skies,
The brown Sierras sharply rise.

This is the haunt of silence; here
Dwells loneliness akin to fear;
And as the stag with agile tread
Crosses that ragged lava bed,
The careful putting of his feet
But makes the stillness more complete.
What means this utter dearth of sounds?
Are these the happy hunting grounds?
Now gracefully the neck of him,
So beautiful, so sleek, so slim,
Bends bowlike, till at last he sips
The crystal tide with velvet lips.
One moment, and the spell is past;
His antlered head on high is cast;
His thin, red nostrils sniff the air,
As though it said to him "Beware!"
A moment thus, and then a quick,
A nervous sound, a warning "click!"—
The four hard hoofs together met
Sharp as a Spanish castanet.
Away! away! at every spring
A shower of pebbles round him ring.
He falls, rolls over—now again
Is rattling down the rocky glen.
Gone like a flash, and silence now
Sifts down from cliff and mountain brow.
The silence grows.   What ailed the stag?
No grizzly looms against yon crag,
Grim, clumsy, ponderous and gaunt;
This is no mountain lion's haunt;
No city hunter with his hound
This rocky fastness yet has found.

Ah, none of these! and yet the deer
Had sudden cause for direst fear,
For yonder, up the rough ravine,
A runner comes, brown, lithe and lean;
A perfect athlete—trained as one
Who in Olympic games would run.
Stark naked, save for sandals tied,
Beneath his feet, thin strips of hide;
Unarmed, save that his fingers clasp
A long, keen knife in bony grasp.
Gods, what a runner! Deep of chest,
And all his muscles at their best—
See how above the skin they rise,
As every move their temper tries!
How free his action! Slightly bent,
His eyes upon the ground intent,
He moves along with easy swing,
A Mercury who needs no wing;
Yet, not too fast, but more as one
Who wins the race before 'tis run.
This is the primal hunter, this
The man whose weapons never miss—
The runner of New Mexico,
Cliff-dwelling Candelario.
His half-starved dog before him goes,
Leading the way with faithful nose.
The stag is doomed, for never back
Turns Candelario from the track.
All day through canyon dark and deep,
Through mountain passes, rugged, steep,
Up walls of rock more wild and sheer
Then ever clomb Swiss mountaineer,

And over plains of scrub mesquite
He follows with untiring feet.
He sleeps upon the trail at night
And starts again at grayest light.
But one such other hunter's name
In all this world is known to fame,
Or e'er was shaped of human breath,
And such a one, I ween, is Death.
He follows so each mortal wight,
So camps upon the trail at night,
Sure that his game, if slow or fast,
Must weary of the flight at last.
Three days are gone since first began
That race between the deer and man,—
A noble course, and nobly run!
The better animal has won.
And now the stag, tired, hungry, weak,
His hair no longer smooth and sleek,
But trickling sweat and dusted gray,
Stands gamely waiting, brought to bay.
His antlered head is bended low,
And near the ground swings to and fro;
His eyes, though shot with streaks of gore,
Blaze fierce defiance all the more.
Not long he waits, for soon there glides
Into the opening where he bides
A naked runner, brown and lean,
Clutching a knife, long, wicked, keen.
Then each the other quickly spies,
And first they wage a war of eyes.
The hunter, bending at the hips,
With twitching hands and parted lips,

Glides watchfully around and round
The stag that turns, but holds his ground,
Disdaining though he often feels
The starved cur snapping at his heels.
Some moments thus, and then at last
The snarling mongrel seizes fast
Upon the deer's hock; mad with pain,
The forest monarch leaps in vain;
He leaps, he stamps, he turns his head—
Swift as a shaft from bowstring sped
The swarthy hunter forward springs;
His left hand to an antler clings,
His right the gleaming weapon wields.
The stag sways to and fro, he yields,
He slowly sinks to earth, his gore
Smokes on the ground, and all is o'er!
And all is o'er, but who would check
The Indian's joy, as on the neck
Kneeling, he swings his knife on high
And wakes the hills with one wild cry?

Three Poets.

THREE poets stood before the king,
  Longing, as poets do, to sing.
The first in clownish garb arrayed,
With jingling bauble ever played;
Over his perky face the while
Flitted a sneer or else a smile.

Well-groomed the second was, and neat,
In proper dress from head to feet;
A mirror of the fashion he,
And ruddy-cheeked, and fair to see.
The third stood near, with drooping head
Unkemmed and pale as are the dead.

"O king, hear me," the first one cried:
"I have no thought on earth beside
To make you laugh, forget your care.
No sacred thing my song shall spare;
Of joy or grief 'tis yours to quaff;
Be wise with me, O king, and laugh."

And thus the second urged his claim:
"Hear me, O king, for I can frame
Ballade, rondeau, and villanelle;
Sonnets by me are finished well,
And I can deftly, truly play
Upon the mocking triolet.

"More tricks I know of phrase and word
Than ever yet by man was heard;
Strange terms, expressions obsolete,
Trip through my lines on dainty feet;
And when the thought seems weak and poor,
I screen it with a phrase obscure."

Slowly the third began to speak;
His voice at first was low and weak,
But soon his words rang clearer, higher,
Until his wondrous eyes caught fire;
And then a light from heaven shed
Sat halowise upon his head.

No leave asked he of court or king;
He sang as those who die or sing:
A strain prophetic, weird, sublime —
The voice and meaning of all time.
Rhymester and clown forgotten lie —
The poet's song shall never die.

An Essay on Fame.

I READ a brilliant essay
   On fame the other day;
The scribe attacked the subject
   In a most decisive way.

She said (for 'twas a woman)
   That glory was a snare,
An ignis-fatuus leading
   Through deadly swamps of care.

She likened it to bubbles
   That tempt the childish eye,
But shatter soon as captured,
   And into nothing fly.

The love of praise, she added,
   Betokened silly pride,
And throve in natures little
   And impudent beside.

But when this witty woman
   Had quite demolished fame,
She closed her brilliant essay,
   And — signed in full her name!

The Rishi.

AN ancient Rishi, legends say,
  A Buddhist of an early day,
His pack of worldly thoughts laid down
And hied him from Benares town.

A chosen spot at length he found
Where naught but nature stretched around,
Where silence reigned supreme, and where
Might penetrate no earthly care.

Content with this, the Hindu sate
Him on the earth to contemplate;
To think away, as Buddhists do,
All passions and all feelings too.

And then, that nothing might surprise
His mind through medium of his eyes,
He fixed those orbs in restful pose
Upon the apex of his nose.

How long he sate there none can tell;
But that he contemplated well
From minor details may be gleaned,
Though ages since have intervened.

For instance, over him a bird
Flew all unnoticed and unheard,
Dropping an acorn as it flew,
Which sprouted as he mused, and grew,

Until his straddled legs between
There stood a shrub of lusty green,

And finally about his head
A mighty oak its branches spread !

Above him squirrels reared their young,
And feathered legions loved and sung,
While all around him, far and wide,
Snakes dug their holes and lived and died.

Of all these things, immersed in thought,
The Rishi knew far less than naught,
Because his vision never rose
Beyond the apex of his nose !

So, wide and far the rumor went,
And many folk in wonderment
Cried, when they saw that face of his :
"How wise a man the Rishi is !"

'Tis but a legend, I confess,
Exaggerated more or less,
And yet within it lurks a seed
Of truth, which all may see who read.

Have we not thinkers, e'en to-day,
Pursuing that old Rishi's way,
Who, deeply learned though they be,
Beyond their noses never see ?

Sunrise on Lake Michigan.

DIM wastes of sea to north and south and west,
Wind-wimpled stretches, steel-gray ere the dawn
Mingled afar with misty, dove-winged skies
That brood and melt and mix until the eye
Knows not where waters end or skies begin.

But in the east, ah, there the wonder is!
High up, the heavens glimmer and grow pale
In awe prophetic of the coming king;
Beneath, for leagues along the watery rim,
A river runs in color like rich wine,
As though the secret cellars of old Spain
Were rifled, and a million vats outpoured.

Upon its farther bank a forest stands
Distinct and dark against the paling sky.
Cloud trees as gloomy as that fabled wood
Where strayed of eld the dismal Florentine.
Deep in such shady sadness one might deem
Old Saturn hid, downcast and desolate,
Dreaming of vengeance 'gainst the traitor gods.
What mighty trunks uplift their branches there,
Waving a night before the gates of Morn!
Great oaks and elms, dense-leaved and vine-o'ergrown,
In random shapes of wildest symmetry.

Now brighter glows the sky; the river runs
A flood of molten sapphire and of sard.
Bright patches fleck the ghostly wood, where flit
Gay butterflies, those living leaves that fall
And flutter from the trees of Paradise.
The river turns to fire, and suddenly,
From trunk to top, through all its gloomy deeps,
The forest blazes forth and burns to naught.

And lo, as new as on the primal morn,
The golden glory of the King of Dawn!

An Improvisation.

HIS hand the master swept along
   The mighty organ's ivory keys,
Waking old memories of song
   And elfin symphonies.

And as he played, a little lute
   That lay unhonored at his feet,
Hearing such strains, could not be mute,
   But thrilled with echoes sweet.

And so, my well-beloved lyre!
   If in these dreamy moods of mine
I strike thee not with godlike ire
   And ecstasy divine,

I'll lay thee down: perchance some time
   Unwooed of me, thy tuneful strings
May tell of melodies sublime
   In truest murmurings!

Ashes.

"TELL me, Age, life's greatest joy,"
   Cried an eager, rosy boy.

"Is it childhood's want of care;
   Boyhood's dream's and visions rare;

Youth's first sip of Passion's wine;
   Manhood's stay at Wisdom's shrine;

Or the calm at set of sun
When the heart repeats, 'Well done'?"

"Ah," Age answered, "Not in these
Life its sweetest pleasure sees;

But in memories of woe
That the heart no more can know."

Wounded Knee.

"GIVE up your rifles!" Stern and clear
    Ring out the words upon the ear.

Yet none of all that motley band
Or moves an eye or stirs a hand.

In silence and disdain profound
Gaze those grim warriors on the ground,

Though round about them ringwise runs
A glittering wall of deadly guns.

What ails those wild and savage men
Hemmed there like cattle in a pen?

Black-haired, high-cheeked and eagle-eyed,
Have they no fear, no hate, no pride?

Ragged they are, and hunger gnaws
The vitals of their sullen squaws.

" Give up your rifles!" Now they look
Like painted Indians in a book.

Each warrior's arms are crossed, and rest,
Beneath his blanket, on his breast.

They make no sign, yet soaring high
Drifts one lone buzzard through the sky.

" Give up your rifles ! " To and fro
Those gaunt forms sway in rhythm slow.

Listen ! What means that guttural moan,
That weird, unearthly monotone ?

" Enough of this ! " The captain's brow
Grows black. " Forward and search them now."

Down drops the buzzard in the blue —
Is that the death chant of the Sioux ?

Quickly, with leveled guns, the men
Step out, the ring contracts, and then —

Red devils, ˡesperate and rash,
Fighting in ragged fire, and crash

Of sudden rifles, sulphurous air,
And lithe fiends leaping everywhere !

Here shakes the dripping tomahawk,
There falls the splintered rifle-stock.

And yonder, with uplifted knife,
The lean squaw writhes amid the strife !

And all is over. White and red
Together piled lie torn and dead.

Now rake the long ravines with shot,
And riddle every hiding-spot !

Let none of them escape, to tell
How many pale-faced warriors fell.

'Tis done, 'twas done; now as we ought
Let us remember how they fought.

Was the Old Guard at Waterloo
Less desperate than those filthy Sioux ?

" Yield you, brave Frenchmen," was the cry ;
" We never yield," they said, " we die ! "

Was Custer, when he fought that day,
More daring and less rash than they ?

Murderous and treacherous at best,
But no slurs 'gainst their courage rest.

I praise them not, I love them not;
But ere their prowess be forgot,

And ere their tribe be dead and dumb,
Oh, that some native bard would come

To sing in weird and worthy strain
Those warriors of wood and plain;

To weave in sad and moving song
The story of their hate and wrong !

Perchance some sweeter time might hear,
And blot the page with many a tear !

The Groggery Cash Bell.

FROM the earliest glimmer of day
　To the setting of every sun,
There's a chiming of bells that merrily tells
　Of shame and of crime begun.
　　Ching !
Five cents for a glass of beer ;
　　Ching !
Ten cents for a whisky straight.
And the devil stands near with a horrible leer
Like the wraith of a hideous fate.

And all through the wearisome night,
　In noisome and smoke-tainted air,
Men are mixing their brains with horrible pains,
　And branding their souls with despair.
　　Ching !
Ten cents for a glass of rye ;
　　Ching !
Fifteen for a Bourbon sour,
While little babes cry because hunger is nigh
And tortures them hour after hour.

Oh, vain for the church bells to sound
　The beautiful praises of Christ.
By a merrier chime ringing all of the time
　Are the souls of our brothers enticed.
　　Ching !
Ten cents for a glass of wine ;
　　Ching !

Fifteen for a bumper of rum ;
While the desolate pine with a patience divine,
 And the mourners with sorrow are dumb.

Then what though hard times be abroad,
 And the gaunt form of Famine appear ?
There is gold and to spare to buy whisky and care,
 And enough to buy sorrow and beer.
 Ching !
Ten cents for insanity's spell ;
 Ching !
Five cents for a bumper of woe —
'Tis a musical knell ringing souls down to hell,
 And to frenzy and shame ere they go !

Sonnets and Ballades.

On Cremation.

IT matters little to the winged sprite
    That flits and flits the clustered stars among,
What fate befell the useless vesture flung
So sadly earthward at the time of flight.
Eyes dazzled by a sudden flood of light
Cannot look into darkness; hymns are sung
In vain for spirit ears on which has rung
God's perfect music heard at last aright.
Yet for this worn-out garment seems more fit
Than beak of Parsee bird, or wormy shroud,
Or grinning ages in Egyptian pit,
A chaunt of merry fire tongues, singing loud,
While deft flame-fingers shall unravel it,
And slim wind-fingers weave it into cloud.

Helen of Troy.

FAINT babbling voices murmur of thy fame,
    Helen of Troy, in chambers of the past;
To us, far off, come clear and loud at last
The growing echoes of thy potent name.
Such splendid image fancy ne'er can frame;

The form divine might be from sculpture guessed,
But who may know what soul the face expressed,
Whose eyes dealt madness in contagious flame?
Old Homer never, with free stroke and bold,
Made vivid painting of thee for our ken.
Of Beauty's prowess 'twas he ever told —
Of dreadful wars, and hosts of maddened men.
Who now can Beauty's subtle charms unfold?
The wars they make reveal them now as then.

George Washington.

HEROIC shadows dimly throng the past;
We hear their hollow voices from afar.
Some stride in ringing mail, and some there are
With graceful togas round their shoulders cast;
Scholars we see, whose eyes have pierced the vast;
Seers that have talked with sphinxes in their time;
And bards renowned, upon whose brows sublime
Sit laurel wreaths that must forever last.
But who is he, yon shade of stately mien,
That, giant-like, in such a throng appears?
We know and love thee, Freedom's greatest son!
A happy nation keeps thy memory green;
For thou art worthy of its splendid years,
And they of thee, O peerless Washington!

Ballade of an Unusual Grief.

I MET Jones on the street t'other day,
And his face was as long as King Lear's;
He appeared in so sorry a way
That he greatly excited my fears.

He'd a look that was wild as a deer's,
    So I asked what had robbed him of rest,
And he answered me, almost in tears,
    "I've a million I cannot invest."

I will own I had felt rather gay
    Till this sorrow assaulted my ears,
But my heart is not marble nor clay,
    And misfortune makes all of us peers.
'Tis not often that any one hears
    Of such trouble, it must be confessed,
And that wail I'll remember for years —
    "I've a million I cannot invest."

There are bards whom the critics all flay,
    And whose verses are greeted with jeers;
There are husbands whose heads have turned gray,
    For the tongues of their wives are like spears;
There are fellows with blighted careers.
    And Death has robbed many a nest;
But why speak of this sorrow with sneers —
    "I've a million I cannot invest?"

ENVOY.
'Tis a world where the sky seldom clears;
    Every life has its sorrow at best —
That of Jones in this sentence appears —
    "I've a million I cannot invest."

Ballade of Bursted Beliefs.

'TIS an era of Science and Doubt;
    Hand in hand, strange to say, they appear,

And how oft they unfeelingly rout
   The beliefs that our fathers held dear !
We are always tormented with fear
   Lest the torchlight of rummaging Truth
May consign some old tale we revere
   To the fables discarded in youth.

For example, historians scout
   And reject, with unanimous sneer,
That delightful narration about
   Captain Smith and the Princess' tear.
William Tell and the cap on a spear
   They declare is a falsehood uncouth ;
And these legends belong, it is clear,
   To the fables discarded in youth.

Now a Frenchman is just bringing out
   Something new in Maid Joan's career ;
'Twill not do his researches to flout,
   For his reasons are cogent and clear.
He declares that she lived to uprear
   A small army of offspring, forsooth !
So the stake we must add, if sincere,
   To the fables discarded in youth.

ENVOY.

Ah, my friends, we are certainly here,
   And we trust in posterity's ruth ;
But our deeds 'twill consign, with a jeer,
   To the fables discarded in youth !

Ballade of the Letter R.

I AM not a great poet, I own;
Nathless my own praise I would sing
In a humble and delicate tone,
And yet with a confident swing.
Pray spare me your pitiless fling,
Nor say I am going too far.
I claim but this one little thing.
I have never made "a" rhyme with "r."

My lines are with nonsense upblown
Till they float without plumage or wing,
And they drop to the earth like a stone
When transfixed by the critical sting.
I have sung on the beauties of spring,
And on themes which most readers debar,
But, in all of my sad maundering,
I have never made "a" rhyme with "r."

'Tis a license that scribblers, high flown,
Bostonese into usage would bring;
But it merits naught else save a groan,
For it gives to their work a false ring.
Of "Maria" and "fire" they may ding,
And may warble of "vista" and "star,"
But this be the stone in my sling:
I have never made "a" rhyme with "r."

ENVOY.

Dear Princess, I own I'm no king;
Among rhymers I'm hardly at par;
And yet to your favor I cling:
I have never made "a" rhyme with "r."

Ballade of Despair.

I'M in love, I am certain, this time ;
    Bear witness my dolorous sighs,
This dejection unfeigned and sublime,
    And the Byronic gloom of these eyes.
Every charm of my darling one tries
    More sweet than the rest to appear,
And my heart in its agony cries,
    Ah me, she is dear, too dear !

All the glow of some tropical clime
    Half hid 'neath her lily skin lies,
But her breath seems to whiten in rime
    When to boldness she calmly replies.
'Twixt passion and distance she flies,
    And I hope, though I tremble with fear,
While these words from my bosom uprise,
    Ah me, she is dear, too dear !

For her sake I would plunge into crime,
    Or with virtue the world would surprise ;
My soul in her cause I'd begrime,
    Or would mount to the star-spattered skies !
But I cannot by any surmise
    Toward the port of her good favor steer,
So I murmur in dolorous wise,
    Ah me, she is dear, too dear !

ENVOY.

She has taken my life for a prize
    Without paying me even a tear,
And my sorrow I cannot disguise —
    Ah me, she is dear, too dear !

A Nobody, Don't y' Know.

THERE'S young Smith — he's a wonder for
    learning :
His attainments are equaled by few ;
He has wit that is quick and discerning,
    And his judgment is solid and true.
In philosophy, ancient and new,
    He knows Zeno as well as Thoreau;
But to call on him hardly would do —
    He's a nobody, don't y' know ?

He can tell, if to hear you are yearning,
    Why the Chinaman first wore a cue ;
He has written a treatise on churning
    As 'twas practiced in ancient Peru.
Of Sturm's theorem he has the clue,
    And can tell you how zoöphytes grow;
But I can't introduce him to you —
    He's a nobody, don't y' know ?

He has published an epic concerning
    The exploits of King Brian Boru ;
He can tell you where Biela's is burning,
    And when Bethlehem's star is next due.
He can sound, like the Swedes can, their "sju,"
    And of tongues has a marvelous flow;
But the Wayups his presence eschew —
    He's a nobody, don't y' know ?

ENVOY.

And the fellow is big-hearted too,
    With a record that's whiter than snow;
But his blood's not sufficiently blue —
    He's a nobody, don't y' know ?

Are They Thankful?

HUMAN nature's a science replete
　With mysteries puzzling and rare,
And these lie the deepest, I weet,
　In the sex that is known as " The Fair."
Why, women are man's dearest care ;
　He protects them in sun and in wet ;
Of all comforts they take lion's share.
　Are they thankful? Well, maybe, and yet—

When it rains and you're out on the street,
　And as fortune will have it, a pair
Of these feminine charmers you meet,
　'Twill not do to pass by with a stare,
Though new is the tile that you wear ;
　You lend your umbrella, and fret
Should a drop either's bonnet impair.
　Are they thankful ? Well, maybe, and yet—

In the street car you capture a seat,
　And you sigh, "I am tired, I declare."
But how often you spring to your feet
　With a suave, Chesterfieldian air,
And a "Madam, be seated, right there !"
　Some thank you, some look their regret,
But they never say no to your prayer.
　Are they thankful ? Well, maybe, and yet—

ENVOY.

There are thousands of instances where
　Women find themselves deeply in debt
To man, though he is "such a bear."
　Are they thankful ? Well, maybe, and yet—

Dante's Story of Francesca.

O FLORENTINE, about whose brows the bay,
  Despite the envious years, twines green and fair,
How oft, in sorrow more than I can bear,
Mine eyes o'erbrimmed, I put thy book away !
Yet, somber poet, when I read to-day
Thy tale of Rimini's unhappy pair,
And saw them wind-whirled in the picture there
Drawn by the matchless pencil of Doré,
I dropped the book and gave a gladsome cry,
As when one feels within his quickened breast
Some new joy's revelation come to dwell.
Oh, Love triumphant ! They go drifting by
In close embrace, with hearts together pressed,
Having each other, and so not in hell.

In Lighter Vein.

IN LIGHTER VEIN.

Ye Bonanza.

IT was a gallant stranger
  Of goodly height and weight,
Who wore a bale of whiskers
  Most fierce to contemplate,
And eke an air of freshness
  Brought from ye Golden Gate.

He came into my sanctum
  One pleasant afternoon,
And hinted that we visit
  Some neighboring saloon.
I made a bad exception,
  And went with him full soon.

When we arrived, ye stranger
  Who hail-ed from ye Coast,
Drew forth a yellow eagle,
  And shouted to mine host:
"Ho! mix us two bonanzas —
  We fain would drink a toast!"

Then did ye skillful mixer
  Two bottles set in line,

Ye one containing brandy,
  Ye other yellow wine ;
And these two pleasant liquids
  Proceeded to combine.

Ye stranger eyed ye compound
  With sigh of deepest bliss ;
Then down his hairy gullet
  It slipped with gurgling hiss,
And I did toss a bumper
  Into mine own abyss.

Then forth again we sallied
  Into ye outer air,
When, lo ! this world seemed glorious,
  This life a boon most rare,
And that bewhiskered giant
  A man divinely fair !

Quoth I : " This same bonanza
  Puts fire into ye heart.
Return with me, I prithee,
  Unto ye liquor mart,
And I, as doth beseem me,
  Will play ye buyer's part."

When next again we sallied
  Into ye crowded street,
'Twas arm in arm we wandered,
  And lifted high our feet,
Ye while ye gracious pavement
  Rose up our soles to meet.

Ye third time that we issued
From that accursed den,
A change was wrought within us
Defying tongue or pen.
Each fire-plug seemed a hogshead,
Each man looked like to ten !

And still a fourth bonanza
Each poured into his face,
Which caused ye mighty buildings
All round about to chase,
And make ye streets and alleys
Tie up and interlace.

Anon ye swaying sidewalk
Grew rife with wriggling things ;
With lobsters, pterodactyls,
And toads with fiery wings ;
With blue and greenish devils,
And snakes with twisting stings.

That night, within ye prison,
I slept as sleep ye dead,
My right arm for a pillow,
An oak plank for a bed ;
And when I woke ye morrow,
I wondered at my head !

Since then, within my pocket
I bear a monstrous gun.
Perchance I may encounter
Again that Native Son ;
And, if he says "bonanza,"
I'll either shoot or run !

Alexander's Poet.

THE other night, while digging out
　　Some bits of ancient truth and slander,
I read a curious tale about
　　The bard of mighty Alexander.

It seems the Conqueror chose to claim
　　God-like Achilles for ancestor,
And with that hero's musty fame
　　His friends he loved to bore and pester.

He had his way, of course ; you see
　　He owned the earth, and it were rather
A shame if such a man as he
　　Could not select his own forefather.

These days an ancient line is bought
　　Often for slight considerations ;
The thing was not with trouble fraught
　　To one who told his wealth by nations.

And when the king had fixed upon
　　The blood from which he drew his glory,
He studied, like a faithful son,
　　To ape his great forefather's story.

And first of all, since he was wise,
　　And fond of reading Homer's pages,
He sought a bard, to advertise
　　His fame to all succeeding ages.

" 'Twas Homer sang Achilles' wrath,"
　　Exclaimed the king; " what modern poet
　Enough of force and frenzy hath
　　To take my louder trump and blow it ?

" Old Homer starved, but he who sings
　　My deeds in half so stately thunder
　Need never fear misfortune's flings,
　　Nor want for earth's most regal plunder.

" But let no common scribbler dare
　　In this great theme to see his mission.
　This is my offer, just and fair,
　　And this its just and fair condition:

" For each good line the bard shall slip
　　Into his purse a mina yellow;
　For each bad verse the whistling whip
　　About his shanks shall make him bellow."

Now want of worth is ever bold,
　　And merit more or less retiring.
　Few bards were tempted by the gold,
　　And less the lashes were desiring.

Of only one tradition speaks —
　　Named Choerilus, a bumptious fellow,
　Who scribbled day and night for weeks,
　　Until his jowls grew thin and yellow.

And when at last his brains ran dry,
　　He rushed before the monarch, crying :
" Rejoice, O king, that bard am I
　　For whom so long thou hast been sighing."

An hour was set, and he began —
   Poor Choerilus ! the sight was funny ;
Upon his left the whipping man,
   Upon his right the man with money.

He read a line, and what a line !
   It wouldn't do; the whip descended.
He read another ; at a sign
   A blow the second sentence ended.

A hundred lines, a hundred blows ;
   A thousand more, a thousand lashes,
Till death relieved him of his woes,
   And turned his hopes and him to ashes.

A tragic tale ; yet tell me, pray,
   Why want should hound each worthy fellow,
And why some bards who write to-day
   Should not be thrashed until they bellow ?

The Man in the Moon.

THE Man in the Moon looked down, looked down,
  As he went sailing over town,
And spied a snug retreat and dark
Beneath a yew tree in a park.
             Oh, dear !
Why did he smile so broad and queer ?

There was a bench beneath the tree,
And on it sat not one nor three,

And yet he peered the branches through
To be quite certain there were two.
    Well, well !
Such tales the Man in the Moon could tell !

He sent a silver shaft of light
Straight through the vague and lying night ;
It flashed athwart two eyes upturned,
And two with love and youth that burned —
    Alack !
And these were blue and those were black.

And then the Man in the Moon sailed past
Across the heavens wild and vast,
And though he smiled, he did not look
Again into that leafy nook.
    Oh ! oh !
He sees so much that's queer, you know !

Some Day — Not Now.

SOMETIME I'll perform such a wonderful deed
 That men will grow breathless and pale when they
  read ;
Some day I'll triumphantly spring with a bound
From the midst of all creatures that walk on the ground ;
And suddenly sprouting my wings, I will rise
To the heavens of fame, the observed of all eyes.
Oh, it makes my pulse throb, and it makes my blood
  warm
When I think of this wonderful deed I'll perform,
    Some day — not now.

Sometime in the beautiful future I'll sing
A song that more clear than a trumpet shall ring;
Some day, when I feel my heart thrill through and
      through·
With love for the lovely, the good and the true,
When my brain is illumined with heavenly ire,
And the wrongs of humanity fill me with fire,
Oh, then I will sing such a magical song,
Such a cry for the right, such a blow at the wrong,
        Some day—not now.

Sometime I will lay all my cowardice by,
And will dauntlessly look the whole world in the eye.
Some day I will dare the false creeds of the hour,
And will bid high defiance to custom and power.
Vain, vain to attack me with sneer or with taunt,
When my black flag you see me courageously flaunt.
Oh, I take off my cap and I drop on my knee,
And I worship the man that I am going to be
        Some day—not now.

Sometime I will suddenly, quietly prove
That a man can jolt out of his natural groove;
Some day I will leave all my follies behind,
All my faults I will scornfully cast to the wind,
Emerging at once from the man I have been,
Like a serpent is said to crawl out of his skin.
Oh, it gives me such comfort to know I shall stand
With those who'll be valiant and noble and grand
        Some day—not now.

Sally.

ACROSS the street there dwells, I weet,
The flower of all the city,
And oh, could I but tell her charms,
The world would sing my ditty !
    Her face is fair,
    And graces rare
Of temper with it tally,
And Fate has granted her to bear
    The dear old name of Sally !

I lurk behind my window blind
For hours in hopes to spy her,
And if I catch the slightest glimpse
It sets my heart afire.
    I swear to you,
    No flower yet grew
In garden or in valley,
And paradise itself has few
    So lovely as my Sally.

Oh, never think her cheeks of pink,
Nor yet her eyes entice me,
For were these all, some other maids
Have charms that might suffice me.
    But in her mien
    Where'er she's seen,
If she's in silk or challis,
There shine the maiden and the queen,
    The worth and grace of Sally !

13

She tries no arts to capture hearts,
And none to kindle passion ;
Her simple truth is lovelier far
Than all the tricks of fashion,
    And Cupid's self,
    The smitten elf,
Near her is fain to dally,
And shoots his shafts no more for pelf,
    But all for love and Sally !

Oh, would she deign o'er me to reign,
With joy I'd be her minion,
And to her slightest wish I'd lend
Anticipation's pinion ;
    But oh, if she
    Unkind should be,
Since I could never rally,
Say this, dear friends, in praise of me :
    " He died for love of Sally ! "

Dr. Wise's Great Theory.

DID you ever hear
    Of old Dr. Wise,
And his theories queer,
    Half fact, half surmise,
Which excited such vast scientific surprise ?
This old Dr. Wise was a wonderful man,
Who mostly to projects and theories ran :
He could tell how a fever-germ acted and grew,
And always could show you a dozen or two,

Tho' the poor devil lying
Fever-stricken and dying
He seldom or never contrived to pull through.
With the greatest presumption
He discoursed of consumption,
And laid all the blame on some parasite sly;
As for cancers and tumors,
They came of bad humors,
And absorption would cause them to shrink up and die.
But this wonderful man not alone
As a common practitioner shone ;
For who has not heard how the whole world was stirred
When he published his book, " The Domestic Outlook ;
Or, How to Exterminate Rats
Without Ferrets or Poison or Cats " ?
Why, the plan was so pretty, so simple and witty,
It seemed a great pity
That rats by the million and billion and trillion
Should haunt human dwellings in country and city.
Just secure a mad cat ;
Let the cat bite a rat,
And there'd be a mad rat ;
There ends *your* labor ;
He'd bite his neighbor,
And then this other
Would poison his brother.
Ah ! I see your face dimple with joy at the scheme.
'Tis as easy and sure as mince pie and a dream.
The madness would spread
Till the last rat was dead.
But 'twas most as a critic that Dr. Wise came
To make for himself a professional name,

For, whenever a patient of wealth or of birth
Would escape his physicians by fleeing from earth,
Dr. Wise never failed to indite a review
Which showed that the death to malpractice was due.
          It is small wonder surely,
            That a man of such skill
            Declared death to be purely
An avoidable ill which ought never to kill.
In fact, he announced it to be his conviction
That death in all cases resulted from friction ;
For the body was naught but machinery cunning,
While life was the power that kept it a-running.
          Then why should not science
            Some cordial distil
            That might bid defiance
            To death's power to kill ?
Some unctuous elixir, to friction superior,
That should lubricate man's complicated interior
Whenever he felt himself grow slightly wearier ?
This argument met on all sides with great favor,
For of reason it really did seem to savor.
Besides, it is true in religion and physic,
When the spirit or body is feeble or is sick,
Man retains best the nostrums of pleasantest flavor.
Or, to hold this thought up to more evident view,
Man accepts as the truth what he'd like to have true.
How many a preacher is salaried well
For a weekly discourse on the absence of hell,
Though his parrot-like lips nothing further can tell !
Now in all human breasts is implanted a strong,
Illogical longing to live, and live long,

Antedating De Leon's historical scramble
Through dangerous wilderness, thicket and bramble,
Over desert and plain and impassable mountain,
To regain his lost years in a mythical fountain.
    The world then received
      Dr. Wise very kindly;
    And ere long it believed
      His great theory blindly.
The excitement produced in a storm culminated,
Into which the famed savant at last fulminated
That he, the invincible investigator,
Had found a receipt for the great lubricator.
Well, to shorten a story already too long,
A hall was secured and a numberless throng,
      The young and the gray,
      The religious, the gay,
Sisters and brothers and fathers and mothers,
Assembled from everywhere, distant and near,
A lecture on "How to Live Always" to hear.
No scoffers were there, their belief was complete,
And each brought a note-book to take the receipt.
Eight o'clock was the hour which the Doctor had set—
Eight o'clock, and he came not; half-past, and not yet
Did his faithful disciples grow weary or fret.
Nine o'clock, and then ten, when, at some one's suggestion,
A carriage was sent for the great man in question.
It went, it returned, and the news quickly spread
That the lecture was off, for the *Doctor* was dead!

Enj'yin' Poor Health.

D'YOU remember Hiram Cawkin,
    Lived in York State years ago ?
Whut a way he had o' talkin',
    How his voice was choked with woe ?
      Allus on the pint o' dyin'
      Allus groanin', gruntin', sighin';
Ask 'im, "Hiram, how's she goin' ?
He'd a kinder knit his brow,
An would answer, lookin' knowin':
      "Thankee,
I'm enj'yin' poor health now."

Wan't 'e long an' thin' an' skinny !
    (No one ever called 'im "tall"—
Allus "long") an' so blame' thin 'e
    Didn't hev no flesh at all !
      Seemed of all ambition lackin',
      'Cept to keep 'is jints a-crackin'
An' to tell the folks 'at met 'im —
Made no diffurnce when er how,
So they paused enough to let 'im :
      "Thankee,
I'm enj'yin' poor health now."

Nineteen year er twenty, is it,
    Sence you last was back in Wayne ?
Year ago I made a visit,
    But I'll never go again.
      Findin' all my friends departed
      Made me feel too heavy-hearted.

Only one man left 'at knew me —
  Hiram Cawkin, an' I swow,
'T sounded good when he sez to me:
    "Thankee,
  I'm enj'yin' poor health now."

Must be ninety, 'f he's two hours,
  Old, y' know when we was young;
Lived on misery.   All 'is powers
  'Round affliction twined an' clung.
    Queer ol' feller; allus groanin,
    Gruntin', whinin', sighin', moanin'.
Soon to glory he'll be strayin',
  'N' I fancy 'im, I vow,
Buttonholin' saints, an' sayin',
        "Thankee,
  I'm enj'yin' poor health now!"

An Obstinate Old Man.

A N old man lived all alone, all alone,
      And a jolly old man was he.
He was ruddy and fat and sleek as a rat,
  And his leg was a good thing to see.
His chest was round, his liver was sound,
  And his voice had a chord of glee
As he sang to himself while he counted his pelf:
        "Oh, ho!
  I'm a hearty and hale old man,
        Ah, ha!
  Such a sturdy and well old man!"

Not a chick nor a child had he in the world,
　　Though his coffers were full of gold ;
He had money in chest, in trousers, in vest,
　　From his pockets the big dollars rolled ;
He owned miles of land and palaces grand,
　　And in bank had thousands untold.
So he sang all the while, with a confident smile,
　　　　"Oh, ho !
　　I'm a likely and pert old man,
　　　　Ah, ha !
　　Such a merry and brisk old man !"

His brothers waited and longed in vain,
　　And for years, I ween, a score,
They would meet each day and pleasantly say :
　　"The old man is right at Death's door."
Then the first one slept, and he never wept,
　　But he laughed and sang the more,
And he gayly cried when the last one died :
　　　　"Oh, ho !
　　I'm a healthy and long-lived man,
　　　　Ah, ha !
　　Such a vigorous, sound old man ! "

Each night his nephews and nieces dreamt
　　Of how rich they were going to grow,
And they loved to hint, " We will never stint
　　When our ship comes in, you know."
But I grieve to tell, he kept hale and well
　　While the years went dragging slow,
And he cackled loud o'er the last one's shroud :

"Oh, ho !
I'm a hardy and stout old man,
Ah, ha !
Such a lusty and tough old man !"

And he's living yet, all alone by himself,
This man I am singing about.
Oh, his eye is bright and his step is light,
And his voice is cheery and stout ;
His cheeks are red and he holds up his head
In a way that puts death to rout,
So I can't see why he should ever die —
Oh, dear !
Such a healthy and well old man,
Ah me !
Such an obstinate, tough old man !

The Roman Nose.

I SING the nose, the kind that grows
Into a huge proboscis ;
The sort that doctors diag-nose
"Elephantiasis naris ossis."
Avaunt, ye folks with tiny snouts,
Of flat, insipid features !
The Muse will none of you ; she scouts
Such ordinary creatures !

I sing the Roman nose — the scythe
That mows its way to glory ;
Sure sign of natures strong and blythe,
Well known in song and story.

On battlefield, in civil life,
  In senate, court and cloister,
The Roman nose is like a knife,
  The world is like an oyster.

The wight whose nose describes a curve
  Like beak of kite or vulture,
Is sure to be a man of nerve,
  And oft is one of culture.
Just cast your eye o'er Clio's page ;
  Research one fact discloses :
The mighty men of every age
  Were men of mighty noses.

Then let us toast the big-nosed host ;
  Let's raise a lusty chorus
Of loud "Amens" from sea and coast,
  Stertorous and sonorous.
And since the promontoried face
  Than others is completer,
God speed the day the human race
  Will shame the great Ant-eater !

Out in Tokio.

EDWIN Arnold, Edwin Arnold,
  Is the story true,
That a little Jap girl
  Has befuddled you ?
All the world is anxious,
  And would like to know,
If you're growing spoony
  Out in Tokio.

Out in Tokio, out in Tokio,
Are you growing spoony
  Out in Tokio?

You, a knight and scholar,
  Lauded to the sky ;
You, a famous poet
  And a C. S. I.;
You, a leader-writer,
  With a wondrous flow,
Courting yellow maidens
  Out in Tokio !
Out in Tokio, out in Tokio,
Courting pudgy maidens
  Out in Tokio !

Such a novel caper—
  Bless us, this is fun !
And they tell us you were
  Born in '31.
Old enough, I fancy,
  Wise enough, I trow,
Not to lose your senses
  Out in Tokio.
Out in Tokio, out in Tokio,
Have you lost your senses
  Out in Tokio ?

Yet the little Jap girls,
  Really are sweet,
With their chubby bodies
  And their dainty feet.

If I weren't so busy
  I would like to go
Giving kissing lessons
  Out in Tokio.
Out in Tokio, out in Tokio,
Teaching osculation
  Out in Tokio.

Love, the wide world over,
  Catches small and great ;
Maidens' eyes are fatal,
  Whether slant or straight.
Hearts were made to open,
  Just as buds to blow.
Luck to bold Sir Edwin
  Out in Tokio !
Out in Tokio, out in Tokio,
Luck to gallant Edwin
  Out in Tokio !

A Song of a Shirt.

[Dedicated to Charles A. Dana.]

I SING the flannel shirt. I would maintain a
    Discussion started first by Charles A. Dana,
Who has so much about the subject squirted
That every one believes him flannel-shirted ;
Though, sooth to say, 'twixt preaching and applying,
There's often fixed a mighty gulf of lying.
Peculiar Dana ! erudite, begoggled ;
Long time has he upon Life's highway joggled,

Making the whole world wonder, as now I do,
When next he'd cut some unexampled dido.
I really hope he'll not get mad and swear, if
I disagree with him about the tariff.
Supporting parties, and their tenets damning,
Is nothing 'cept the keenest kind of shamming.
There's many another odd, fantastic caper
He's cut from time to time, in his great paper.
For instance, when so boastfully he blustered
About the merits of a king of mustard
Proposing for the presidential mansion —
A Western trust's obscure and feeble stanchion.
Then, too, I always fancied there was harm in
His queer ideas anent the art of farmin'.
But why waste time and paper scribbling railings
At such a good and great man's petty failings ?
When after ages have forgot his blundering,
His mighty name shall still go grandly thundering
Adown the years, a snowball waxing greater,—
The flannel shirt fad's first originator.
Then yield him present fame ; much weal to him an'
    his ;
Oft may his pole reach first where the persimmon is.
When summer days are muggy, moist and torrid,
And salty rills run down the tickled forehead ;
When ironed collars scratch the smarting gullet
Until it's rough and red as any mullet,
Or ridge about the neck 'till one is dull, sure,
Who sees in man no semblance to a vulture ;
When pious folk, in fact, observe no sin in
Wishing to hades everything that's linen,

Immortal Charles! I think of thee.   Then fancy
Comes with her weird, ecstatic necromancy,
And pictures thee in skies of glory sailing,
Thy flannel shirt about thee coolly trailing!
Hence these poor lines.   Oh, damn them not with
    laughter —
I seek to seize the tale and follow after.

A Confession of Love.

I'M in love with a widow.   I own it.   I swear it!
    Fill your glasses, and drink me her weal.
Ridicule, disaffection — let none of you dare it;
    Real love is too precious, and my love is real.

But first, jolly friends, ere you hasten to pledge her,
    Of her virtues I'll briefly descant;
Everything that is charming I'll boldly allege her —
    "More virtues than virtue?"   Ah, well, that I'll
        grant.

As a comrade, my widow's seductively sprightly;
    Nature made her, and then made no more;
Hours of transport I spend in her company nightly;
    I have ceased but to love, I'm a slave, I adore!

The first kiss that I give her deliciously thrills me,
    And the next shoots a glow to my heart,
But the madness that finally seizes me, fills me,
    Makes me fear my sweet witch, while I bow to her
        art.

Yet why should I fear her? She fills me with daring,
  With great purpose and lofty resolve;
She transports me beyond all annoyance's wearing;
  In her smile all my troubles, like vapor, dissolve.

She's kind-hearted, my charmer; for, swayed by her
      magic,
  I am friendly with lover and foe;
And if any man loves her, he'll not find me tragic,
  For my widow, dear friends, is the widow Cliquot!

High Tea at Mrs. Rhynde's.

[See Horace Satires, ii., viii.]

DID you attend the high tea of Mrs. Bacon Rhynde?
    No? Well, you missed such splendor as you will
    seldom find.
The hostess spared no trouble to make it *recherché*,
And what in taste was lacking was made up in display.
A canvas from her portico extended to the street,
And rich and costly carpets were spread beneath the
    feet;
A gorgeous costumed footman first helped us to the
    ground,
Then waved us to the front door, with salaam most
    profound;
But, once within the mansion, such splendor met the
    gaze
That one might well give vent to some courteous amaze
In little "ahs" and "lovelys," that meagerly expressed
The admiration great of each newly entered guest.

But all the decoration had nothing to compare
With the flowers in profusion, seen blooming every-
 where.
Round grates and lofty mirrors they seemed to trail
 and bloom ;
From rich and costly vases they shed a faint perfume ;
From crystal chandeliers they were pendant overhead.
The whole scene was a wonder of green, and white, and
 red.

'Mid all the festal brav'ry the hostess moved, elate,
In rustling silks and laces, in splendid jeweled state ;
Her fat and jolly features bedewed with beads of sweat,
Her very dress in places with perspiration·wet ;
While little founts of moisture sprung from her
 shoulders and
Ran trickling through the powder, like brooklets
 through the sand.
Her costume was a marvel, and every one confessed
The lady was most richly and wonderfully dressed.
The epaulettes of ribbon that from her shoulders
 flapped
The climax of her costume appropriately capped.
To add to all this grandeur, and make it just *au fait*,
Tight clasped in bulging gauntlets she held a big
 bouquet.

But now I know you wonder who at the hostess' side
Stood ready to assist her, her labors to divide.
Two young and lovely ladies were to this task
 assigned —
Miss Esmerelda Rashyr, Miss Eva Bacon Rhynde.

The guests at last are gathered, and round the table
 placed,
Discussing tea and gossip, with well-developed taste.
A woman's pretty mouth's not unlike Pandora's box,
For out of it, when opened, misfortunes fly in flocks.
In tenderest female bosoms good names are doomed to
 death,
And foulest tales are wafted at first by sweetest breath.
So these good ladies soon turned the wasps of scandal
 loose,
And, while they praised the hostess, took notes for
 future use.

But who composed this throng, of such wit and beauty
 rare ?
I cannot name them all, for the *élite* all were there.
No common Smiths and Joneses were in that stylish
 crowd,
But Sybyl Smythe was present, and those de Joneses
 proud ;
With Mrs. Randolph Baykyr was Miss Estella Close,
And Georgianna Roset—her uncle's name is Rose.
Minna de Longe was there, too, bejeweled, *decolleté*—
Her name was Molly Long once, so cruel gossips say.
Her father took to dredging, and made his pretty pile ;
To boarding-school went Mary, and stayed a little
 while ;
A grub she went away, but a butterfly became—
Too fine a thing by far for a common, vulgar name!
And I must not forget sweet Geralde de Vincent
 Stubs—
Her mother, Lucy Stubb, once bent over washing-tubs ;

Nor must I pass Miss Blacke by, nor fair Blanche
    Hyggynstone,
Who scorn the Blacks and Higgins, and disdainfully
    disown !

Oh ! magic god of Mammon ! For, in so brief a while,
These haughty titles blossom beneath thy potent smile.
And, oh ! this fruitful country, this strong, young land
    of ours,
Where honor grows so fast when refreshed by golden
    showers !
Ancestors, crests and heirlooms — we need no thousand
    years :
Give us a little money, and how soon the rest appears !

Our hostess was most eager that none should fail to see
How quite aristocratic was her mode of serving tea ;
And, lest some little detail should lack admiring eyes,
She talked of this and that, and solicited replies.
Whene'er her language failed, or her meaning scarce
    expressed,
Miss Rashyr or Miss Rhynde would interpolate the rest.
She said she hoped her guests would excuse her if she
    tried
To show how things were managed "upon the other
    side ;"
That she was just from Yurrip, and meant soon to go
    again,
Where she took observations among the "upper ten."
Miss Rasher then remarked that the flowers were
    gorgeous, very.
"They all came," said the hostess, "from my conserva-
    terry."

Here Miss Rhynde hoped the cake's taste was equal to
    its look,
As it was made by their new ten-thousand-dollar cook.

And now our hostess gave us a genuine surprise :
Our ears she next delighted, as well as taste and eyes.
From out a bower of roses there came a dulcet din —
The band was led, she told us, "by Signor Mandolin."
But yet our entertainment by no means was complete ;
It seems she still had for us reserved a mental treat.
She introduced a young man, Professor Lawrence Brays,
And said he'd read us something from "Mr. Shakes-
    peare's plays."
But here an interruption inopportune occurred —
A servant entered, boldly, as one who will be heard,
And said : "Plaize, mum, there's waiting below, widin
    the dhure,
A dapper little fellow, who says you'll see him, sure.
He sthripped his hat an' coat off, as handy as you please,
An' says, 'I'm ripresintin' the Daily Mornin' Breeze.'"
"Oh dear ! it's a reporter," the hostess cried in grief ;
" I do declare, such boldness almost exceeds belief.
I shrink from public notice, 'tis such a vulgar thing ;
Send him about his business with his reportering."
"Indade, he'd not uv passed me," chimed Patrick in
    with vim,
"Had not the lyin' spalpeen tould me you sint for him."
At this a muffled titter broke out, but quickly died,
While Mrs. Rhynde most sternly the stupid servant eyed.
In fact, a pause quite awkward fell on the gathering gay,
Until Miss Rashyr went down to send the wretch away.

But, ah, the sly reporter! he's made of eyes and ears;
For in this morning's daily a full account appears.
"Aristocratic Splendor," the screed is headed so,
And all the decorations are mentioned high and low;
The list of guests is given, the costumes that each wore,
While all throughout, the hostess is lauded o'er and o'er.

But hours of merry-making fly from us wondrous fast,
And even so much splendor could not forever last.
The ladies speak of leaving; 'round Mrs. Rhynde they
    press
To say they've had such pleasure as words cannot express.
Another interruption, however, mars the scene,
And clothes with sudden thunder the hostess' brow
    serene.
For Mr. Clarence Rhynde, in his shirt-sleeves and his
    hat,
Rushed in, exclaiming, "Here, now, what are you women
    at?
I know that mother told me to keep myself away,
But f'r all these fancy fixin's I have the bills to pay.
I want ye to feel welcome, an' so I've had a team
Drive 'round from Sweetner's, loaded with candy an' ice
    cream.
Don't scowl so at me, mother; I guess I know my biz;
I feel like celebratin', for, mother, pork is riz!"

As near as I remember, that's all you'd care to hear;
And yet this brief description is very poor, I fear.
To Mrs. Rhynde's next high tea you mustn't fail to go;
Just change your name to Smythe and she'll look you
    up, I know.

Thanksgiving Thoughts.

THANKSGIVING THOUGHTS.

The Agnostic.

I DO not know whom I should thank,
   And if I thank the wrong one,
Who'll save me, 'tis a query frank,
   From anger of the Strong One ?

So I will live and go my way,
   Like other things are going,
And save my thanks until a day
   When I become more knowing.

The Materialist.

O PRINCIPLE of Life, that lives
   About all things, and through and through;
Most penetrating Power, that gives
   Old things the grace to change to new !

Which shall I praise and honor most,
   The wave that ever ebbs and swells,
Or Nature's vast and varied host,
   In which this essence sweetly dwells ?

The Very Poor Man.

I THANK Thee, Lord, that I have strength
To work a day of any length.
I thank Thee, also, that the powers
Have not increased my working hours;
That shelter, clothing, food and fire,
Though high enough, are not still higher;
That so few babes my household bless
(I would have been content with less).
I thank Thee that my wife is strong
And works to help us get along.
I thank Thee that my girl and boy
Have in the factory found employ,
And only work ten hours a day—
I wonder if they sigh for play?
I thank Thee for myself and wife
That there's an end some time to life.

The Purse-proud Man.

O LORD, I thank Thee for my wealth
And all the blessings which it buys:
The joys of travel, freedom, health,
And power that even law defies.
Learned though I am not, when I speak,
Applause attends, and deference meek.

Fair women woo me with their smiles;
Perhaps they love not—who can tell?
So sweetly skillful are their wiles,
Deception pleases me as well.

I enter halls of wealth and pride,
And worth and honor stand aside.

I thank Thee, Lord, that all my life
Thy special favor hovers o'er,
Guarding it well from vulgar strife.
And, Lord, I do respect Thee more
That Thou hast had the wit to see
The difference 'twixt the mob and me.

The Moderate Man.

FOR life and hope and sweet content,
For heavenly favors justly sent,
For honest toil and its reward,
I thank Thee, Lord.

Because no foolish lust for praise
Makes more than wretched all my days,
Nor threatens sleep with sword of flame,
I bless Thy name.

For children, home and faithful wife,
For all the joys of simple life,
For freedom from desires abhorred,
I thank Thee, Lord.

Because I am not rich nor poor,
Because no beggar shuns my door,
And no proud man my soul can tame,
I bless Thy name.

The Christian.

GOD of the wooing spring,
  Of pregnant summer, fertile fall,
And winter, wrapped and slumbering ;
I hear Thy voice when linnets sing,
Or brooding thunders hoarsely call ;
I see Thy hand in everything,
Guiding and shaping all.

God of the perfect year,
God of the living and the dead,
'Tis Thee I thank with grateful tear
For purple grape and yellow ear,
And all these blessings round me spread ;
I am Thy child, well known and dear ;
From Thy hand I am fed.

Should sorrow come, or pain,
I still would magnify Thy name.
In blighting drought and saving rain,
In wealth increased, and labor vain,
In honor, station, or in shame,
Thy purpose works, obscure or plain ;
Thy wisdom lives the same.

Translations.

TRANSLATIONS.

Horace to Dellius.

[Liber ii., Carmen iii.]

B E brave in trial and in pain ;
    With placid mind thy griefs defy,
And let not Fortune make thee vain,
    O Dellius, for thou must die.

Whether thy life must all be sad,
    Or days of festive joy be thine,
While grassy lollings make thee glad,
    And draughts of old Falerian wine.

Where giant pine and poplar white
    Weave lovingly their wooing shade,
And where the rill takes mazy flight
    With silvery laughter down the glade,

There order wines and perfumes sent,
    With sweet rose blooms too quickly fled,
While life and youth to thee are lent,
    And ere the dark Three snap thy thread.

Thou must depart that villa fair,
    Those lawns by tawny Tiber's side ;
Thou must depart, and then an heir
    With thy vast wealth will glut his pride.

Art rich, and sprung from ancient kings?
Or poor, and made of vilest clay?
No difference such distinction brings,
For all are cruel Orcus' prey.

The same end waits for all; or late
Or soon thy lot must leave the urn,
When Charon's bark must be thy fate—
An exile, never to return.

Tout la Lyre.

[After Victor Hugo.]

WITH all trials Thou hast tried me,
        O my God!
I have known not where to hide me
        From the rod.
I have sinned not, yet my guerdon
        Is sharp pain;
I am with my daily burden
        All but slain.
Disappointment's fiery lashes
        Smite me sore,
And my honors seem but ashes
        At the core.
I have plowed in bitter weather,
        Sown in tears,
And have seen my worst foe gather
        All the ears.
With my fame have Malice, Frenzy
        Had their way,
Like the lean-ribbed tigress, when she
        Rends her prey.

I have dreamed so much, my reason
  Turns to doubt.
Jealousy has with its treason
  Found me out.
I have searched, pale-faced, forsaken,
  Heaven's dome,
While my dead were being taken
  From my home.
Do such sorrows make me curse Thee —
  Woes like these ?
Nay, O God, I laud Thy mercy
  On my knees ;
For my heart, however riven,
  Seared with pain,
Has ne'er loved and not been given
  Love again !

To be a Poet.

[From the French.]

TO be a poet ? 'Tis to love
  The soul in nature that reposes ;
  The sun, Love's self, the fragrant roses,
And all sweet things below, above.

To be a poet ? 'Tis to feel
  Infinity within thy breast ;
  To suffer with the world's oppressed,
And prove with deeds thy sorrow real.

To be a poet ? 'Tis to sigh
  With hope that life devotes, sublimes ;
  To suffer death a thousand times,
And then at last never to die !

Horace to Chloe.

[Liber i., Carmen xxiii.]

CHLOE flees me like a fawn
For its timid mother running,
Into pathless mountains gone,
Every wind-stirred thicket shunning.

Let a bush but feel a breeze,
Or green lizard in it shaking,
And the timid creature's knees
And her breast with fear are quaking.

I'm no Afric lion, dear,
No fierce tigress, you to harry :
Leave your mother and your fear ;
You are old enough to marry.

To Love Indeed.

[From the Greek Anthology.]

SAY not "I love," when Beauty storms,
And takes perforce thy willing heart ;
Her kindling smile each bosom warms,
Her eye is Cupid's bow and dart.
For rosy cheeks and breasts of snow,
And teeth that gleam where red lips be,
Such things will drive men daft, you know,
As long as men can think or see.

But if a passion in thee rise
  For one whose outward look is bad,
Then dost thou see with partial eyes;
  Then love indeed hath made thee mad.

  For scented breath and laughter low,
    And thrilling eyes of gray or jet—
  All men must yield to these, you know,
    As long as suns shall rise and set.

Cupid Sleeping.

[From the Greek Anthology.]

THROUGH a shady forest going,
  Found we Cupid all alone,
And his cheeks, so smoothly glowing,
  Like to golden apples shone.

He had not his quiver by him,
  Nor his bow well-bent and strung;
But we soon espied them nigh him,
  'Midst the leafy branches hung.

Chains of sleep his limbs encumbered,
  While among the flowers he lay;
Smiling, even when he slumbered,
  In his cruel, roguish way.

Swarms of tawny bees came flying
  All about his waxen lip—
Often thus one sees them trying
  Flowers that with honey drip.

15

The Broken Vase.

[From the French.]

THE vase where this vervain is dying
　　Was cracked by a fan lightly swayed,
By a blow that was surely not trying,
　　And that scarcely a sound-tremor made.

But the seemingly harmless beginning
　　Has eaten the crystal each day
With progress invisible, winning
　　Round the glass its insidious way.

Drop by drop its fresh water is going,
　　Which the flowers revived and awoke ;
The fissure is there, no one knowing :
　　So touch not the vase ; it is broke.

Thus carelessness oft, when a lover's,
　　Wounds the heart, though it utter no cry ;
Thus it breaks of itself, nor recovers,
　　And its flowers of sentiment die.

Its appearance, no doubt, is deceiving,
　　But it grieves o'er the one wounded spot,
While it feels itself secretly cleaving —
　　It is broke, it is broke, touch it not !

Premier Sourire du Printemps.

[From the French of Gauthier.]

WHILST the stubborn human race
  Is intent upon its sinning,
March, who laughs in Winter's face,
  Slyly plans the spring's beginning.

Round the dainty Easter daisies,
  While the dreaming world is still,
Cunningly the fringe he raises,
  Shapes each golden ball with skill.

He's to Nature, as I take it,
  Chief hair-dresser, and with fine
Snow he fills his puff, to shake it
  Over tree and whitened vine.

Now she in her couch reposes;
  He is in the garden seen
Lacing tight the coy young roses
  In their corset's velvet green.

Now and then a sweet wind-ditty
  To the merl he whistles low;
Here and there his hands the pretty
  Violets and snowdrops sow.

By the fountain side he lingers;
  Where the shy stag drinks he dwells,
Opening with unseen fingers
  Lily-of-the-valley bells.

He is hiding in the meadow
　　Strawberries of vermeil hue;
He is weaving coolest shadow
　　From the sun to shelter you.

Soon his labors' end discerning,
　　Knowing that his reign is o'er,
Toward April's threshold turning,
　　Cries he: "Spring, come out of door!"

Angel and Child.

BESIDE a cradle for a space
　　An angel paused and bent to look,
And seemed to see his own pure face
　　As in the mirror of a brook.

"Dear child, that so resemblest me,"
　　He sweetly said, "ah, come away.
Together we shall happy be;
　　Thou art too good on earth to stay.

"There is no perfect bliss below;
　　For even pleasure has its sting,
Each song of gladness chords of woe,
　　Each joy its sigh of suffering.

"Oh, then, must trouble and must fears
　　Impair the beauty of thy brow?
Must sorrow dim with bitter tears
　　Those eyes, where heaven is shining now?

"No, no. The flowery firmament,
The fields of glory for us wait;
Tow'rd thee doth Providence relent,
 And saves thee from an earthly fate.

"Let none wear mourning in thy home,
For all should be as glad, dear child,
This day that bids thy spirit roam,
As when thy blue eyes earliest smiled.

"Let no face there show sorrow's sign;
Let no one deck the house for death;
For when the soul is white as thine,
The latest is the happiest breath."

And speaking thus, the angel wide
His snowy pinions waved, and fled
To where the pure for aye abide.
Poor mother, see, thy babe is dead!

Hymn to Aphrodite.

[From the Greek of Sappho.]

Translations of this, the most complete of the Sapphic fragments, have been made by Ambrose Phillips, 1711; by Herbert, 1713; by Edwin Arnold, 1869; by John Herman Merivale, 1833; by T. W. Higginson, 1871; by J. Addington Symonds, 1883, and by others. The exquisite finish and divine frenzy of the Lesbian poetess can never be even hinted at. Even Swinburne has failed in his celebrated "Sapphics," though he has made a most creditable effort.

SPLENDOR-ENTHRONED, divine Aphrodite,
Daughter of Zeus, wily weaver of snares,
Crush me not, goddess, with agony mighty;
Hear these my prayers.

Haste now, if ever thy heart has grown tender
    When I have called to thee, calling afar ;
Come now, as erst, from the home of thy splendor,
    Yoking thy car.

Fair are thy sparrows, with well plumèd pinions,
    Fleetly all round the dark planet they flew,
Whirling thee swift through the azure dominions,
    Out of the blue.

Sudden they brought thee, but thou, O Divinest,
    Smiling, with countenance lovely for aye,
Spak'st to me, saidst to me: "Daughter, why pinest ?
    What dost thou pray?

"Tell me thy frenzied heart's fieriest longing.
    Yearnest some love-luring charm to possess ?
Who hath neglected thee, who hath been wronging ?
    Sappho, confess.

"For if he fly, he shall seek thee in anguish.
    Scorns he thy gifts ? He shall offer his own.
Scorns he thy love ? He shall soon for it languish,
    Though it be flown."

Speed to me now, goddess, loose me from sorrow ;
    Grant my fierce yearnings fruition and end.
Thou art all potent; thy strength would I borrow.
    Oh ! be my friend.

Resignation.

[From the Swedish of Vitalis.]

WHY should I not meet Grief in joyous fashion ?
    It is God's angel and should welcome be.
Why should I doubt my Father's kind compassion
    Because he sends stern messengers to me ?

Like timid bird beneath its mother's pinions,
    Close to his breast I creep in hiding sweet,
And though Death seek me with a thousand minions,
    My faith itself is victory complete.

Like some mild pigeon winging from its sender,
    My prayer has pierced the starry realms above,
And, flitting whitely through his perfect splendor,
    It takes this message to his heart of love :

I yield my will to Thee.   Do not disdain it,
    O Thou whose eyes into my heart can see.
Lo ! lovingly I seize Thy cup and drain it,
    Just as in love Thou reachest it to me !

Sir Butterfly's Wedding.

[From the French.]

AROUND the Parson's gate
    A merry throng await
Sir Butterfly, the popular and gay.
  " Marry ! " they shout together,
  " For you in pleasant weather
Have courted every pretty flower of May."

The spruce young celibate
Replied : " How can I mate ?
I have no house where wife and I could live."
" My son, that doesn't matter,"
Cries Snail above the clatter,
" For I have one that I will freely give."

The roguish celibate
Still asks : " How can I mate ?
My bed without a single sheet would be."
But Spider, sitting in
His star, replied, " I'll spin,
And you shall have a plenty, you will see."

The roguish celibate
Still asks : " How can I mate ?
There'd be no bread for wife and me to eat."
Now, Ant enjoys a joke,
And laughingly he spoke :
" If bread is what you lack," said he, " I'll treat."

Again the celibate
Replies : " How can I mate ?
Dry bread is rather unattractive fare."
" For wine, rely on me,
For I've a pantry key,"
Says Mr. Rat, " and rummage everywhere."

The roguish celibate
Yet asks : " How can I mate ?
I think we'd need a little sugar, too."
" Do what your friends advise,"
'Tis Honey Bee replies,
" You're welcome to my honey, and 'twill do."

The roguish celibate
Still says : " How can I mate ?
I haven't e'en a cent to buy a light !"
But Glow-worm cries : "Oho !
My friend, I'd have you know
That with my lantern you'll not think it's night."

" Oh, yes," the victim whined,
" Let's give, since you're inclined,
A wedding without music, by all means."
" Aha !" exclaim the Crickets,
" There'll be a rush for tickets
To hear our cymbals and our tamborines."

The poor old celibate
Entered the Parson's gate,
And made the due arrangements like a child.
His friends all kept their word,
But after mass was heard
They plagued him till they nearly drove him wild.

Honolulu.

[From Sarah Bernhardt's French.]

HONOLULU 'S the gem of the ocean ;
Mid the tear-jeweled billows she lies,
And aye on their languorous motion
She dreams with her beautiful eyes.

Her bed is of seaweed ; red roses
The walls of her sky overcreep ;
And there in the mist she reposes,
Lulled to rest by the waves of the deep.

Rocked to rest by the waves that are dying,
　Soothed asleep by the low lullaby
Of palm and of cocoa trees sighing
　To the winds from the sea and the sky.

Her odorous winds are a-shiver
　With the wings of a musical throng,
And the reeds by the sea-reaches quiver,
　And are loud with the voices of song!

There is passion, and daring, and lightness
　In the heart of this queen of the West,
And she smiles on the waves with the brightness
　Of a siren when charming her best.

And the hoary old sea-cliff, whose duty
　Is to watch o'er the bride of his vows,
Gazes jealously e'er on the beauty
　And the light-hearted joy of his spouse.

Honolulu's a pearl, and they found her
　In the azure-hued brine, where she lies
With the winds and the waves gathered round her,
　And above her the innocent skies.

But see!　O'er the shimmering water
　Comes the satin-robed dawn in her shell;
I am off on the billows that brought her—
　Honolulu, farewell, oh, farewell!

Laplander's Song.

[From the Swedish of Franzen.]

L EAP, my swift reindeer,
    Over plain and hill !
Thou shalt browse thy fill
My love's hut a-near.
Softest mosses grow
There beneath the snow.

Ah, how brief the day,
And the road how long !
Leap thou with my song ;
Let us haste away.
Here can be no rest ;
Wolves this place infest.

See yon eagle rise —
Ah, that I could fly !
See yon cloud scud by —
Would I sailed the skies,
So I from above
Might behold thee, Love !

You so quickly yet
Firmly trapped me, Sweet !
So the wild deer's feet
Find the snare that's set.
Oh, my life seeks thine
Like yon stream the brine !

Each succeeding sun,
Each slow night that wears,
Brings its thousand prayers —
Thousands, yet but one —
Just this prayer alone,
That thou be mine own.

Under bowlders steep
Thou mayst hide in fear,
Or with fleet reindeer
Flee to forests deep :
Rock and stately pine
Stay not love like mine !

Leap, my swift reindeer,
Over plain and hill !
Thou shalt graze thy fill
My love's hut a-near.
Sweetest mosses grow
There beneath the snow.

The Stinger Stung.

[From the Greek of Theocritus.]

LOVE, the thief, chanced on a day
    Near the bees to linger,
When a naughty one, they say,
    Stung him on the finger.

Oh, the wound, it hurt him so !
    How he blew and shook it !
How he stamped and danced with woe,
    Then to mother took it.

Spreading all his fingers, he
　Sobbed to Aphrodite :
"Mother, little is the bee,
　But its sting is mighty ! "

Then the Queen of Passion smiled,
　And she answered merely :
" You are small yourself, my child,
　But you wound severely."

The Milky Way.

[From the French of Sully Prudhomme.]

UNTO the stars I said one night:
　　" Ye are unhappy, as I deem.
Your rays, so softly, meekly bright,
　Through boundless spaces sadly stream.

"And oft I fancy that ye go
　Like white-clad mourners through the sky,
With myriad virgins holding high
　Their torches in procession slow.

" Live ye one ceaseless life of prayer ?
　Is grief with your existence wed ?
For these are tears of light most fair,
　Not rays of glory, that ye shed.

" O ancient stars, that lived and shone
　Ere gods or creatures filled the years,
Within your eyes are bitter tears."
　They answered me : " We are alone !

"Each one of us is very far
    From all her sisters seen by thee ;
Our beams no messengers can be
    Of what we feel or what we are.

"And cold, unfeeling space devours
    The final warmth of every ray."
I said : "I know what ye would say,
    For ye are like these souls of ours.

"For they, like you, with friendly light
    Their sisters seem to warm and bless,
Yet in eternal loneliness
    They burn in silence and in night."

If Animals Could Speak.

[From the French.]

I WOULD not wrong the human kind,
    Though I've but scanty faith in it ;
Yet in my La Fontaine I find
    That brutes have often shrewdest wit.
We all love sayings bright and new,
    And (not my fellow-man to pique)
Perhaps they wouldn't be so few
    If animals could only speak.

For instance, take the sorry hacks
    That pull a street-car o'er the stones ;
All day the driver swears, and cracks
    His lash about their smarting bones.

In hot and cold, in wet and snow,
  They toil and suffer, patient, meek ;
Some new profanity we'd know
  If animals could only speak !

Whenever through the streets you see
  His course some hapless blind man feel,
His little dog is sure to be
  Somewhere anear him, watchful, leal.
In every eye for pity's tear,
  The brute's eyes, longing, seem to seek ;
True eloquence we oft might hear
  If animals could only speak !

In summer nights the kind moon shines
  On many a lonely country road,
The lover then throws down the lines
  And tightly holds his buxom load.
The horse looks back and sees — ah, well !
  It brings the blushes to my cheek
To think what stories he could tell
  If animals could only speak.

The cook below delights to flirt
  With her policeman by the hour ;
That's why she ruins the dessert,
  And why the bread is always sour.
Beneath the stove the tabby sleeps
  With one eye open, fat and sleek ;
He'd show how faithful tab he keeps
  If animals could only speak !

I think it's time that I were done ;
My muse grows clumsy in its feet .
(For diagram that goes with pun,
  Address 620 Bogus Street.)
I greatly fear my friends will say :
" That poet's brain is waxing weak —
The ass would rhyme in just that way
  If animals could only speak !"

A Night in Lesbos.

Λέδυκε μὲν ἀ σελάννα
κὰι Πληΐαδες, μέδαι δέ
νύκτες, πάρα δ' ἔρχετ' ὥρα,
ἔγω δὲ μόνα κατεύδω.
          — *Sappho, 52d Fragment.*

THE moon has left the sky,
  The Pleiades are flown,
Midnight is creeping nigh,
  And I am still alone.

Ah me, how long, how long
  Are all these weary hours !
I hate the night-birds' song
  Among the Lesbian flowers.

I hate the soft, sweet breeze,
  That comes to kiss my hair
From oleander trees
  And waters cool and fair.

My heart is fierce and wild ;
  The winds should rave and moan ;

Ah, why is nature mild
When I am here alone ?

While yet the silver moon
Rode o'er the laughing sea,
My heart was glad, for, "Soon,"
I said, "he comes to me."

But when its placid sphere
Slid swiftly 'neath the wave,
I sighed : "He is not here ;
Be brave, my heart, be brave."

Then for an age of woe,
Of doubts and hopings vain,
I watched the white stars snow
On yon Ægean plain.

I named them by their names,
Alcyone and all,
Those far and happy flames,
On which we mortals call.

" Ere that one sets," I said,
" My soul shall swim in bliss ;"
And then, "Ere that is fled
My lips shall feel his kiss."

The moon has left the pole,
The Pleiades are flown,
'Tis midnight in 'my soul,
And I am here alone !